DATA COMMUNICATION AND COMPUTER NETWORK

EASY TO LEARN AND SIMPLE TO DEVELOP

Dr. M.P. VANI

Associate Professor
School of Information Technology
Department of Software and System Engineering
Vellore Institute of Technology
Vellore

INDIA • SINGAPORE • MALAYSIA

Notion Press

Old No. 38, New No. 6
McNichols Road, Chetpet
Chennai - 600 031

First Published by Notion Press 2019
Copyright © Dr. M.P. Vani 2019
All Rights Reserved.

ISBN 978-1-64587-658-8

This book has been published with all efforts taken to make the material error-free after the consent of the author. However, the author and the publisher do not assume and hereby disclaim any liability to any party for any loss, damage, or disruption caused by errors or omissions, whether such errors or omissions result from negligence, accident, or any other cause.

While every effort has been made to avoid any mistake or omission, this publication is being sold on the condition and understanding that neither the author nor the publishers or printers would be liable in any manner to any person by reason of any mistake or omission in this publication or for any action taken or omitted to be taken or advice rendered or accepted on the basis of this work. For any defect in printing or binding the publishers will be liable only to replace the defective copy by another copy of this work then available.

Contents

Preface   7
Acknowledgements   11

UNIT – I   13

Chapter 1 Introduction   15
    1.1 Data Communication Introduction   15
    1.2 Data Representation   16
    1.3 Data Flow   17
    1.4 Networks   18
    1.5 Physical Structure   19

Chapter 2 Layered Tasks   25
    2.1 The OSI Model   26
    2.2 Layered Architecture   27
    2.3 Peer-to-Peer Process   27
    2.4 Interface Between Layers   27
    2.5 Encapsulation   29

Chapter 3 TCP/IP Protocol Suite   32
    3.1 Introduction to TCP/IP Protocol Suite   32
    3.2 Purpose of TCP/IP Protocol Suite   32
    3.3 Physical Layer   35
    3.4 Data Link Layer   35

UNIT – II 37

Chapter 1 Physical Layer and Media 39
1.1 Data and Signals 39
1.2 Analog and Digital Signal 40
1.3 Periodic Analog Signal 41
1.4 Sine Wave 41
1.5 Peak Amplitude 41
1.6 Time and Frequency 42
1.7 Phase 42
1.8 Length 42
1.9 Bandwidth 43

Chapter 2 Transmission Impairment 44
2.1 Attenuation 44
2.2 Distortion 44
2.3 Noise 45
2.4 Data Rate Limits 45
2.5 Noiseless Channel: Nyquist Bitrate 46
2.6 Noisy Channel: Shannon Capacity 46
2.7 Bandwidth in Bits Per Second 47

Chapter 3 Multiplexing 48
3.1 Multiplexing 48
3.2 Transmission Media 50
3.3 Fiber Optic Cable 53
3.4 Spread Spectrum 54
3.5 Spread Spectrum Concept 55

UNIT – III   57

Chapter 1 Switching   59
   1.1 Circuit Switched Network   60
   1.2 Data Transfer Phase   61
   1.3 Packet Switched Network   61

Chapter 2 Datagram Network   64
   2.1 Routing Table   65

Chapter 3 Virtual Circuits Networks   67

Chapter 4 Structure of Switch   70

UNIT – IV   75

Chapter 1 Data Link Layer   77
   1.1 Data Link Layer Error Detection and Corrections   77
   1.2 Performance of Simple Parity Check   81
   1.3 Check Sum   82
   1.4 Cyclic Redundancy   84
   1.5 Random Access Method   87
   1.6 Multiple Access   88
   1.7 Channelization   90
   1.8 TDMA: Time Division Multiple Access   92

UNIT – V   97

Chapter 1 Network Layer   99
   1.1 IPV4 Addresses   99
   1.2 Structure of IPV4 Address   101

Chapter 2 IPV6 — 103
  2.1 IPV6 Address — 103
  2.2 Multicast Address — 105
  2.3 Process-to-Process Delivery — 106

UNIT – VI — **109**

Chapter 1 UDP (User Datagram Protocol) — 111
  1.1 User Datagram — 111
  1.2 Check Sum — 112

Chapter 2 TCP — 113
  2.1 Goal of TCP Congestion Control — 113
  2.2 Closed-Loop Congestion Control — 114
  2.3 Choke Packet — 115
  2.4 Explicit Signalling — 115

UNIT – VII — **117**

Chapter 1 Application Layer — 119
  1.1 Telnet — 120
  1.2 FTP — 121
  1.3 SNMP — 122

Chapter 2 Quality of Service (QoS) — 124

References — *127*

Preface

Data Communication and Networking is considered as the rapid growing technology in our todays values one of the implications of that development is a intense increase in the number of professions, where the technologies essential for the success are understood and a fair increase in the number and types of students taking course to learn about them. Various description of the text are designed to make it particularly easy for students to understand data communication and networking.

Data communication and computer network are changing the way to do business and the way we live. Business today relay on computer networks and internetworks. We need to know how network operate, what type of technologies are available and which design best fills which set of needs.

A Network is a combination of hardware and software that transmits data from one location to another. The hardware consists of physical equipment that carries signals from one point of the network to another. The software consists of instruction set that make possible the services that we expect from a network. The main function of the physical layer is to transmit data in the form of electromagnetic signals across a transmission medium. Computer network is designed to send information from one point to another. This information needs to be converted either a digital signal or an anolog signal for transmission.

In real life we have link with limited bandwidth. Bandwidth has been and will be one of the main challenges of electronic communications sometimes it becomes necessary for us to combine several low-bandwidth channel to make use of one channel with larger bandwidth. Sometimes we need to expand the bandwidth.

Unit-I Gives the overview of data communications based on data representation, flow of data and physical structure. It uses concepts of layered tasks at the sender and receiver site, how exchange is done using OSI model. It introduces TCP/IP protocol suite it shows how it differs from OSI model.

Unit-II It deals with physical layer media using Analog and digital signal and bandwidth used in larger channel.

Unit-III It deals with switching concepts and data transferred using packet switched Network, datagram network, network routing table, and structure of switch.'

Unit-IV It concentrates on data link layer, Error detection and correction, Random access method, checksum and TDMA concepts.

Unit-V It emphasis one Network layer, it concentrates on addresses like IPV4 addressing and IPV6 addressing techniques.

Unit-VI Concepts based on UDP, TCP, Congestion control and choke packet techniques are implemented.

Unit-VII Highlights on application layer based on FTP, Telnet, SNMP and quality of services are concentrated.

Computer network can be divided into various types such as Client Server, Peer-to-Peer or hybrid depending upon its architecture. Computer systems and peripherals are connected to form a network. They provide various advantages of resource sharing, exchange of information through e-mails and FTP, web or internet, IP phones, Video conferencing, parallel computing Instant messaging.

Acknowledgements

I thank the management of Vellore Institute of Technology Dr. G. Viswanathan Chancellor, Mr. Sankar Viswanathan, Vice President A.P. campus, Dr. Sekar Viswanathan Vice President Vellore Campus, Mr. G.V. Selvam Vice President Chennai Campus, Dr. Sandhya Pentareddy Executive Director Dr. Anand A. Samuel Vice Chancellor, Dr. S. Narayanan Pro Vice Chancellor Dr. K. Sathyanarayanan Registrar for their Inspiration and encouragement in bringing out this book.

I am grateful to Dr. Balakrushna Tripathy Dean School of Information Technology, Dr. Sree Dharinya S Head of Department of Software and System Engineering, my colleagues and staff members VIT for their assistance and support.

I am highly indebted to my publisher Mr. Naveen Valsakumar, Ms. Nikita Pre publishing Manager, my Publishing Manager Ms. Dhanya, and the staff of Notion press for the effort taken for bringing out this book.

I acknowledge the continuous support, assistance and encouragement given by my parents and my sons Hari Prasad and Sridhar, who have made this time of writing pleasant and enjoyable.

UNIT - I

CHAPTER 1
Introduction

1.1 Data Communication Introduction:

Data communications are the exchange of data between two devices through some form of transmission medium such as wire cable.

*for data communications to occur the communicating devices must be part of communication system made up of combination of hardware (physical equipment) and software (programs)

Characteristics of data communication:

*data communication consists of four characteristics:

 i. **Delivery:** The system must deliver data to correct destination.

 ii. **Accuracy:** The system delivers the data accurately.

 iii. **Timeliness:** The system must deliver the data in a timely manner. (real time transmission)

 iv. **Jitter:** Jitter refers to variation in the packet arrival time.it is the uneven delivery of audio or video packets.

For e.g. let us assume that the video packets are sent every 30 ms. If some of the packets arrive within 30 ms. delay and other with 40 ms delay leads to uneven quality in the video.

1.2 Data Representation:

Data representation information comes in different forms such as text, numbers, images, audio and video.

Components: data communication has five components

1. **Message:** the message is the information (data) to be communicated. Popular forms of information include Text, numbers, pictures, audio and video.

2. **Sender:** the sender is the device that sends the data message. It can be computer, workstation, telephone handset, video camera and so on.

3. **Receiver:** the receiver is the device that receives the message. It can be computer, workstation, telephone handset, television and so on.

4. **Transmission Medium:** it is a physical path by which a message travels from sender to receiver for e.g. twisted pair wire, coaxial cable, fibre optic cable and radio waves.

Text: Text is as a bit pattern a sequence of bit (0's or 1's). Different set of big pattern s have been designed to represent

Numbers: numbers are also represented as a bit pattern.

- Number is directly converted to a binary number to simplify mathematical operation.

Images: images are also represented by bit patterns

- it is composed of matrix pixels
- each pixel is a small do
- the size of pixel depends on the resolution

For e.g. image can be divided into 1000 pixels or 10,000 pixels.

Only black and white 1 bit pattern.

For 4 levels of grey pixels 2 bit pattern.

A black pixel is represented by 00.

A dark grey pixel is represented by 01.

A light grey pixel is represented by 10.

A white pixel is represented by 11.

There are several methods to represent color images on.

one method is called RGB and another method is called YCM.

Audio: Refers to recording or broadcasting of sound on music.

Video: Refers to recording or broadcasting of picture on movie.

1.3 Data Flow:

Communication between two devices can be simplex, half-duplex or full Duplex

Simplex:

- Communication is uni-direction as one way street.
- Only one of two devices on a link can transmit the other can only receive. E.g. Keyboard and Traditional monitors.

Half-Duplex:

- In half duplex mode each station can both transmit and receive, but not at the same time. When one device is sending the other can only receive.

- It is like one lane road with traffic allowed in both direction.

- No need of communication at the same time e.g. walkie-talkie and CB (citizen band) radios are both half-duplex system.

Full-Duplex:

- Full-duplex mode (also called duplex), both stations can transmit and receive simultaneously.

- It is like two way street with traffic flowing in both directions at the same time. e.g. Telephone network.

- The capacity of the channel must be divided between the two directions.

1.4 Networks:

- Network is a set of device (referred as Nodes) connected by communication links.

- A node can be a computer, printer, or any other device capable of sending and receiving data generated by other nodes of the Network.

Network Criteria: the important criteria are performance, Reliability and security.

i. **Performance:** performance is often evaluated by two networking metrics throughput and delay.

ii. **Reliability:** in addition to accuracy of delivery network, reliability is measured by the frequency of failure.

iii. **Security:** protection of data from unauthorized access, protecting data from damage and development.

- Implementing policies and procedures for recovery from breaches and data losses.

1.5 Physical Structure:

Types of connection

i. Point-to-point

ii. Multipoint

i. Point-to-Point:

A point to point connection provides a dedicated link between two devices

- Most point-to-point connections use an actual length of wire or cable to connect the two ends.

ii. Multipoint:

A multipoint (also called Multidrop) connection is one in which more than two specific devices share a single link.

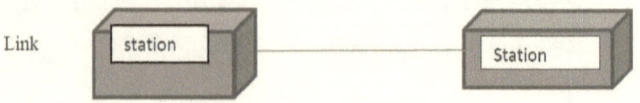

Figure 1: Point-To-Point

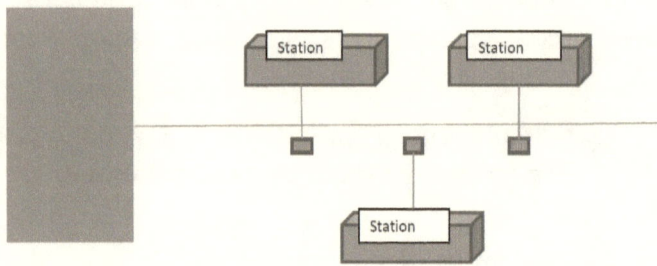

Figure 2: MultiPoint

Physical Topology:

The term physical topology refers to the way in which a network is layered out physically.

- The topology of network is the geometric representation of the relationship of all the nodes.

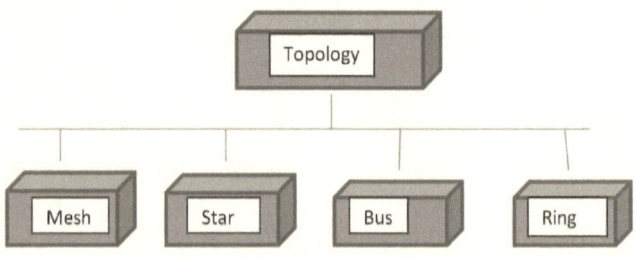

Figure 3: Physical Topology

Mesh:

- it has a dedicated point to link to every other device.

- node 1 must be connected to n−1 node, node 2 must be connected to n−1 node and finally node n must be connected to n−1 node.

- if each physical link allows communication in both direction (duplex node) we can divide the number of links by 2.

$n(n-1)/2$

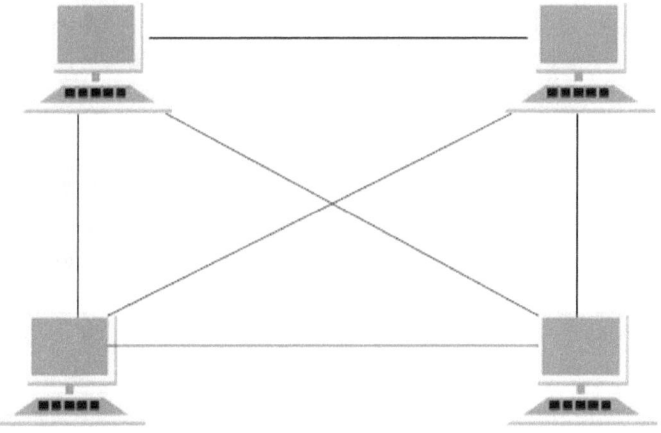

Figure 4: Mesh Topology

Advantage of Mesh:

1. It eliminates traffic problems.

2. It is robust, if one link fails it uses the next link.

3. There is advantage of privacy and security.

Disadvantage of Mesh:

1. every device must be connected to every other device.
2. bulk of wiring can be greater than the available space.
3. hardware required to connect each link can be expensive.

Star Topology:

- Each device has a dedicated point to link. Only to a central controller usually called a hub.
- Unlike mesh topology star topology does not allow direct traffic between devices (star topology used in Lan).

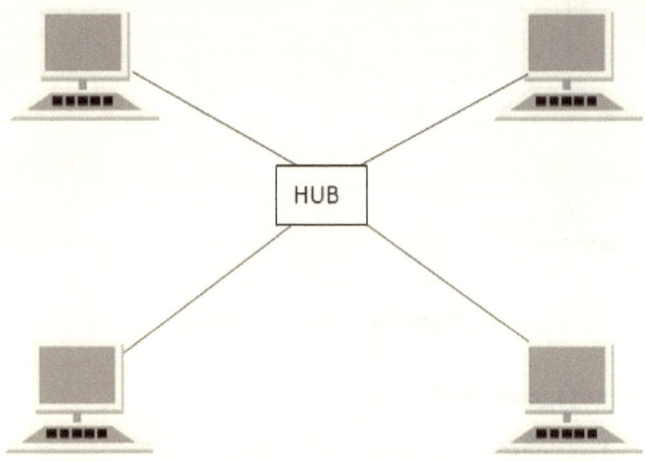

Figure 5: Star Topology

Advantage:

1. Less expensive.
2. Robustness if one link fail only that is affected. All other link remains active.

Disadvantage:

1. Dependency of the whole topology is on one single point the hub. If the hub goes down the whole system is dead.

Bus Topology:

- Bus topology is a multipoint.
- One long cable acts as a back bone to link all the devices in a network.
- Nodes are connected by drop lines and taps.
- Drop line is a connection running between the device and the main cable.
- A tap is a connector that either splices into the main cable or punctures the sheathing of a cable, to create contact with metallic core

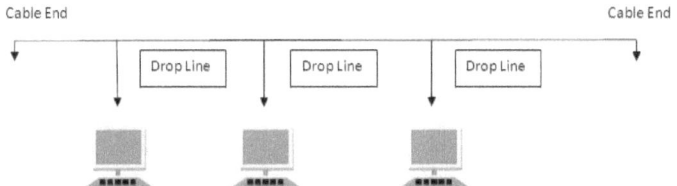

Figure 6: Bus Topology

Advantage:

1. Easy installation.
2. Cable redundancy is eliminated only back bone cable stretches through the entire facility.

Disadvantage:

1. Difficult reconnection and fault isolation.

CHAPTER 2

Layered Tasks

We use the concept of layers in our daily life for e.g. let us consider two friends who communicate through postal mail. The process of sending a letter to a friend would be complex if there were no services available from the post office.

Sender, Receiver and Carrier:

We have a sender, receiver and a carrier that transports the letter. There is a hierarchy of tasks.

At the Sender Site:

- **Higher Layer:** the sender writes the letter in an Envelope, writes the sender and receiver addresses and drops the letter in a mail box.

- **Middle Layer:** the letter is picked up by a letter carrier and delivered to the post office.

- **Lower Layer:** The letter is sorted at the post office, a carrier transports the letter.

On the Way: on the way to the recipients local post office, the letter may actually go through a central office. In addition it may be transported by tuck, train, airplane, boat or a combination of these.

At the Receiver Site:

- **Lower Layer:** The carrier transports the letter to the post office.
- **Middle Layer:** The letter is sorted and delivered to the recipients mailbox.
- **Higher Layer:** The receiver picks up the letter opens the Envelope and reads it.

Services: Each layer at the sending site uses the services of the layer immediately below it.

- The sender at higher layer uses the services of the middle layer. The middle layer uses the services of the lower layer. The lower layer uses the services of the carrier.
- The layered model that dominated data communications and networking literature before 1990 was the open system Inter connection (OSI) model
- Ever one thought that OSI model will become ultimate but this did not happen.
- TCP/IP protocol suit became the dominant commercial architecture.

2.1 The OSI Model:

- The OSI model was established in 1947.
- It is an International Standard Organization.
- The purpose of OSI model is to show how to facilitate communication between different systems without changing the logic of the underlying hardware and software.
- The OSI is not a protocol.

- It is a model for understanding and designing network that is flexible, robust and interoperable.

2.2 Layered Architecture:

The OSI model consists of 7 layers, Physical layer (1), Data Link layer (layer 2), network (layer 3), transport (layer 4), session (layer 5), presentation (layer 6), application (layer 7).

*The communication between machine is done in a given Layer called Peer-to-Peer process.

2.3 Peer-to-Peer Process:

A sends a stream of bits to device B (through Intermediate nodes) A the higher layer.

- Communication must move down through the layer on device A over to device B. and then backup through layer.
- Each layer in the sending device adds its own information to the message it receives from the layer just above it and passes the whole package to the layer just below it.

For e.g. layer 2 removes the data meant for it then passes the rest to Layer 3 then Layer 3 removes the data meant for it and passes the rest to layer 4 and so on.

2.4 Interface Between Layers:

- The transferring of data and network information down through the layers of the sending device and backup through the layers of the receiving device is made possible by interface between each pair of adjacent layers.

Organization of the Layers:

- The 7 layers can be thought of as belonging to 3 subgroups layers 1, 2 and 3- physical, data link, and network are the network support layers.

- They deal with the physical aspects of moving data from one device to another.

- Layers 5, 6 and 7 session, presentation, and application can be thought of as the user support layer.

- Layer 4, the transport layer, links the two sub groups and ensures that what the lower layers have transmitted in the form of upper layer.

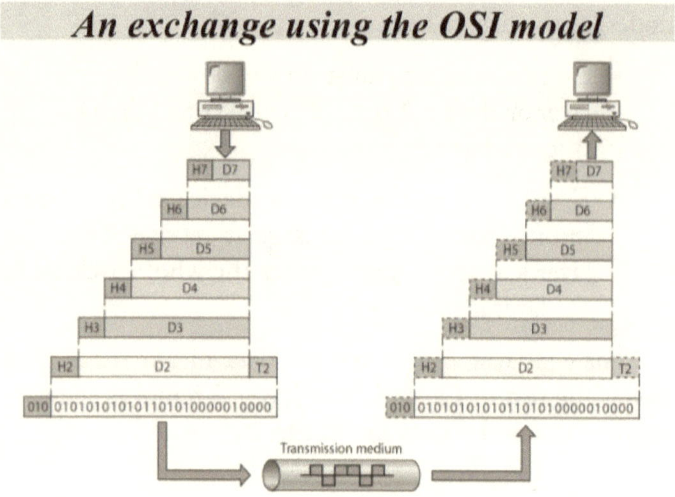

An exchange using the OSI model

Figure 1: An exchange using OSI model

- It gives a overall view of the OSI layer.

    D7-> Data unit at layer 7

    D6->Data unit at layer 6 and so on

The process starts at layer 7 (application layer) then moves from layer to layer in descending sequential order.

- At each layer a header, or trailer can be added to the data unit.

- Commonly the trailer is added only at layer 2.

- When the formatted data unit passes through the physical layer (layer 1) it is changed into an electromagnetic signal and transported along a physical layer.

- Upon reaching its destination the signal passes into layer 1 and is transformed back into digital form.

- The data units then move back up through the OSI layers.

- As each block of data reaches the next higher layer the headings and trailers attached to it at the corresponding sending layer are removed and the action appropriate to that layer is taken.

- By the time it reaches layer −1 the message is again in a form appropriate to the application and is made available to the recipient.

2.5 Encapsulation:

- A packet (header & data) at level 7 is encapsulated in a packet at level 6. The whole packet at level 6 is encapsulated in a packet at level 5 and so on.

- The data portion of a packet at level N−1 carries the whole packet (data and header and may be trailer) from level N is treated as one integral unit.

Layered Task:

- One whole network process is divided into small tasks.
- Each small task is assigned to a particular layer.
- It works dedicatedly to process that task only.
- Each layer does only specific task.
- In layered communication system one layer of a host deals with task done by or to be done by its peer layer at the same level in the remote host.
- The layer is either initiated by later at the lowest level or at the top most level.
- If the task is initiated by the top most layer it passed on to the layer below it or for further processing.
- The lower level layer does the same thing it processes the task and passes on to lower layer.
- Every layer joins together all procedures, protocols and methods which it requires to execute its piece of tasks.

OSI Model:

- OSI model is open system interconnect is an open standard for all communication system.
- It is established by international standard organization

Application Layer: It provides interface to the application user

- It contains protocols which directly interact with user.

Presentation Layer:

- Defines how data in the native format of remote host should be presented in the native format of host.

Session Layer:

- Maintains session between remote hosts for e.g. once user/password authentication is done the remote host maintains this session for a while and does not ask for authentication again in that time spam.

Transport Layer:

- This layer is **responsible** for end-to-end delivery between hosts.

Network Layer:

- Responsible for address assignment and uniquely addressing hosts in a network.

Data Link Layer:

- For reading and writing data from and onto the line.
- Link errors are detected at this layer.

Physical Layer:

- This layer defines the hardware, cabling, wiring, power, output, pulserare etc.

CHAPTER 3
TCP/IP Protocol Suite

3.1 Introduction to TCP/IP Protocol Suite:

The TCP/IP protocol suite do not match exactly with the OSI model.

TCP/IP is thought of as a five layer model.

Comparison between OSI and TCP/IP

OSI	TCP/IP
All seven layers are present	Session layer and presentation layer are missing.
Each layer serves separate purposes	The application layer is considered as the combination of three layers in the OSI model.

Figure of TCP/IP

3.2 Purpose of TCP/IP Protocol Suite:

- TCP/IP suite is a small private internet.
- Such an internet is made up of several small network which we call links.
- A link is a network that allows a set of computers to communicate with each other.

4	8	16		32
Ver.	IHL	Type of service	Total length	
Identification			Flags	Offset
Time to live		Protocol	Checksum	
Source address				
Destination address				
Option + Padding				
Data				
Structure of the IP header in 32 bit lines.				

4	8	16	24	32
Ver.	Priority	Flow label		
Payload length		Next header	Hop limit	
Source address (128 bites):				
Destination address (128 bites):				
Structure of the IPv6 header in 32 bit lines.				

16	32
Source port	Destination port
Sequence number	
Acknowledgement number	
Offset | Reserved | U | A | P | R | S | F	Window
Checksum	Urgent pointer
Option + Padding	
Data	
Structure of the TCP header in 32 bit lines.	

The TCP/IP and OSI Models

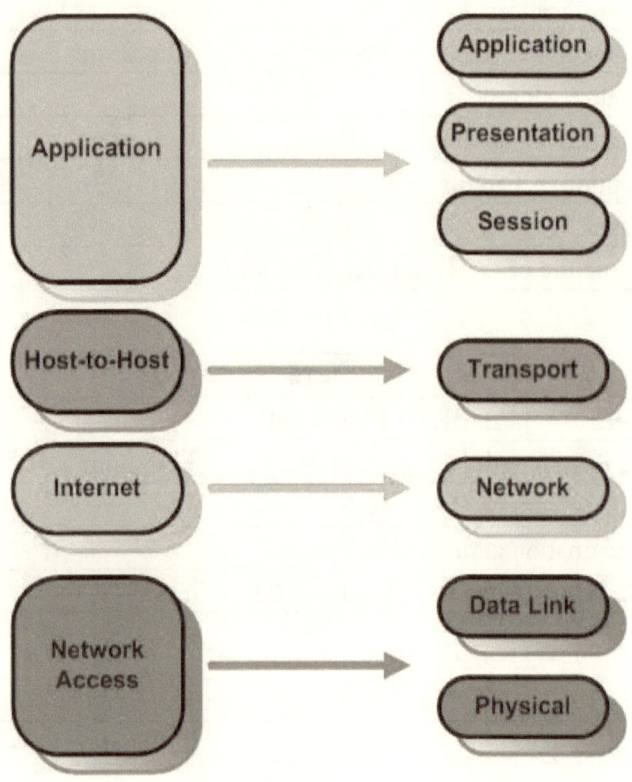

Figure 1

For e.g.,

If all computer belonging to a private company are connected via a satellite channel, the connection is a link

- A link can be LAN or WAN.
- We also assume that different links are connected together by devices called router or switches.

- **Fig:** shows imaginary internet that is used to show the purpose of each layer. We have 6 links and four routers (R1toR4).

3.3 Physical Layer:

- TCP/IP does not define any specific protocol for the physical layer.

- The communication between two hops or nodes either a computer or a router.

- The unit of communication is a single bit.

When the connection is established between the two nodes a stream of bits is flowing between them.

- The physical layer treats each bit individually.

- A journey of bits between computers A and computers B is mode of 4 independent short trips.

- Computer A sends each bit to router R1 in the format of protocol used by link1.

- Router1 sends each bit to router R3 in the format dictated by the protocol used by link 3 and so on.

3.4 Data Link Layer:

- TCP/IP does not define any specific protocol for the data link layer.

- The communication take place between two hops or nodes.

- The unit of communication is a packet called frame.

- A frame is a packet that encapsulates the data received from the network layer with an added header and sometimes a trailer.

- The head includes the source and destination of frame.

- The destination address is needed to define the right recipient of the frame because many nodes have been connected to the link.

UNIT - II

CHAPTER 1
Physical Layer and Media

- The physical layer has complex tasks to perform.
- One major task is to perform services for the data link layer.
- The data in the data link layer consists of 0's and 1's organized into frames that are ready to be sent across the transmission medium.
- One of the major task is to provide signals services for the data link layer
- The data in the data link layer consists of 0's and 1's organized into frame ready to be sent across the transmission medium.
- The transmission medium is a passive entity
- It has no logic program or control like other layers
- The physical layer on the number of logical channels for transporting data coming from different sources.

1.1 Data and Signals:

- One of the major function of the physical layer is to move data in the form of electromagnetic signals across transmission medium.

- Let it be either collecting numerical statistics from another computer, sending animated pictures or causing a bell to ring it all rely on transmission of data across the network connection.

- Transmission media work by conducting energy along a physical path.

1.2 Analog and Digital Signal:

- Signal can be either Analog signal or digital signal.

- In Analog the waves moves from value A to value B it passes through and includes an infinite number of value along its path.

- A digital signal can have only limited number of defined values as simple as 1 and 0.

- The simples way to show signal is by plotting them on a pair of perpendicular axis.

- The vertical axis represents the value or strength of a signal.

- The horizontal axis represents time.

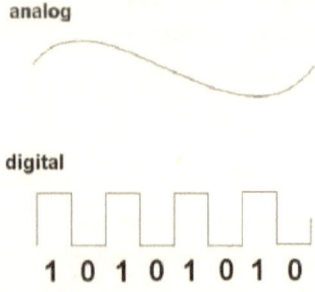

Figure 1: Analog and Digital

- The curve represents Analog signal passes through an infinite number of points.
- The vertical line of the digital signal demonstrates te sudden jump that the signal makes from value to value.

1.3 Periodic Analog Signal:

- It is classified as simple or composite.
- A simple periodic Analog signal a sine wave cannot be decomposed into simpler signals.
- A composite periodic Analog signal is composed of multiple sine waves.

1.4 Sine Wave:

- The sine wave is the most fundamental form of a periodic Analog signal.
- When we consider it as simple oscillating curve, it's change over the course of a cycle is smooth and consistent, a continuous rolling flow.

In the fig. each cycle consists of a single arc above the time axis followed by a single arc below it.

- A sine wave is represented by three parameters the peak amplitude, the frequency, and the phase.

1.5 Peak Amplitude:

- The peak amplitude of a signal is the absolute value of its highest intensity, proportional to the energy it carries.

- For electric signals, peak amplitude is normally measured in volts.

1.6 Time and Frequency:

- Time refers to amount of time in seconds signals need to complete one cycle.
- Frequency refers to the number of periods in I's.
- Period is the inverse of frequency and frequency is the inverse of period.

  $f = 1/T$ and $T = 1/f$

  period is formally expressed in secs. Frequency is formally expressed in Hertz (HZ) which cycle per second.

1.7 Phase:

- It describes the position of the waveform relative to time 0.
- If we think the wave as something that can be shifted forward or backward along the time axis phase describes the amount of that shift.
- Phase is measured in degrees or radians [3600 is 2 n rad; 10 is 2n/360 rad and 1 rad is 360/(2n).

1.8 Length:

- It is another characteristic of a signal travelling through a transmission medium.
- Wave length binds the period or frequency of a simple sine wave.

- Wave length describes the transmission of light in an optical fibre.

- Wave length is represented by Lambda Propagation speed by C (speed of light) and frequency by f.

  Wave length = propagation speed *period =

  Propagation speed/frequency

- The wave length is normally measured in micrometres (micron) instead of meteor.

1.9 Bandwidth:

- The range of frequencies contained in a composite signal is its bandwidth.

- Bandwidth is the difference between two numbers.

For e.g if a composite signal contains frequency between 1000 and 5000 its bandwidth is 5000–1000 or 1000.

CHAPTER 2: Transmission Impairment

- Signal transfers through transmission media which are not perfect.
- This means the signal caused at the beginning of the medium is not same as the signal at the end of the medium.

2.1 Attenuation:

- It means loss of energy.
- When a signal sample or composite travels through a medium it loses some of its energy in converting the resistance of the medium.
- That is why a wire carrying electrical signal gets warm if not hot for a while.
- To compensate this loss amplifiers are used.
- Attenuation are measured in terms of Decibels

  $dB = 10 \log P_2/P_1$

  variable p1 and p2 are the powers of the signal points.

2.2 Distortion:

- It means the signal changes its form or shape.
- It can occur in a composite signal made of different frequencies.

- Each signal component has its own propagation speed.
- Differences in delay may create a differences in phase if the delay not exactly the same as the period duration.

2.3 Noise:

- It is another cause of impairment.
- Noise are of several types such as thermal noise, induced noise, cross talk, and impulse noise may corrupt the signal.
- These devices act as a sending antennae, and the transmission medium acts as the receiving antenna.
- Cross talk is the effect of one wire over the other.
- One acts as a sending antenna the other is acting as a receiving antenna.
- Impulse noise is a spike (signal with very high energy in a very short time) that comes from power line lightening and so on.

2.4 Data Rate Limits:

Data rate depends on 3 factors:

1. Bandwidth available
2. the level of signals we use
3. the quality of the channel

2.5 Noiseless Channel: Nyquist Bitrate:

Bitrate = 2*bandwidth * 10g2L

-bandwidth is the bandwidth of the channel.

-L is the number of signal levels used to represent data and Bitrate is the bitrate in bits per second.

- when we increase the number of signal levels.
- if the number of levels in a signal is just 2 the receiver can easily distinguish between a 0 and a 1.
- if the level of signal is 64, the receiver must be very sophisticated to distinguish between 64 different levels.
- increasing the level of signal reduces the reliability of the system.

2.6 Noisy Channel: Shannon Capacity:

- Shannon introduced a formula called Shannon capacity.

  Capacity = bandwidth xlog2 (1/SNR)

  - Bandwidth is the bandwidth of the channel.
  - SNR – is the signal-to-noise ratio.
  - Capacity – capacity is the capacity of the channel in bits per second.

2.7 Bandwidth in Bits Per Second:

- The term bandwidth can also refer to the number of bits per second that channel link or even network can transmit.

For e.g. one can say the bandwidth of a fast Ethernet network is a maximum of 1000 Mbs i.e., network can send 100 Mbs.

CHAPTER 3
Multiplexing

3.1 Multiplexing:

Multiplexing is the set of techniques that allows simultaneous transmission of multiple signals across a single data link.

- the lines on the left direct their transmission streams to a Multiplexer (MUX) which combines them to a single stream (Many-to-one) at the receiving end.

- at the receiving end the stream is fed into DE multiplexer (DEMUX) which separates the stream back into component transmission. (one to many)

- the link refers to physical path.

- the channel refers to the portion of a link that carries transmission between a given pair of lines.

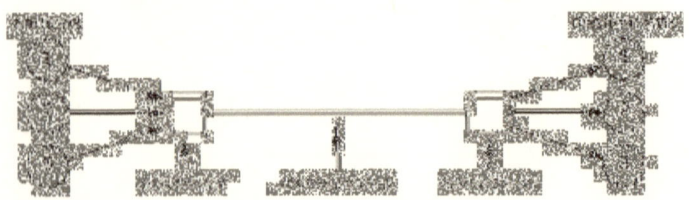

Figure 1: Multiplexing

Three Basic Multiplexing Technique:

1. **Frequency-Division Multiplexing**
2. **Wave-Length division Multiplexing**
3. **Time-division Multiplexing**

The first two techniques are designed for Analog the third of digital signal.

1. Frequency Division Multiplexing:

- FDM is an Analog technique.
- it can be applied when the bandwidth of a link (in hertz) is greater than the combined bandwidth of the signals to be transmitted.
- these modulated signals are then combined into a single composite signal that can be transported by link.
- carrier frequencies are separated by sufficient bandwidth to accommodate the modulated signal.
- bandwidth ranges are the channel.
- channels can be separated by strips of unused bandwidth guard bands to prevent signals from overlapping.
- carrier frequency must not interfere with original data frequencies.

2. Wave Length Division Multiplexing:

- (WDM) is designed to use high-data-rate capability of fibre optical cable.

- optical fibre data rate is higher than the data rate of metallic transmission cable.

- fibre-optic cable for single line wastes the available bandwidth.

- multiplexing allows us to combine several line into one.

- WDM is same as FDM except the Multiplexing and Demultiplexing involve optic signals transmitted through fibre optic channels.

3. Time Division Multiplexing:

- TDM is a digital process.

- allows several connections to share the high bandwidth of line instead of sharing a portion of the bandwidth.

- same link is used in FDM.

- we are concerned with only multiplexing not switching.

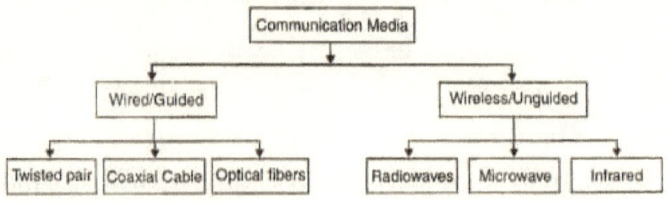

3.2 Transmission Media:

- A transmission medium can be broadly defined as anything that can carry information from a source to a Destination.

For e.g. the transmission medium for two people having a dinner conversation is the air. The air can also be used to carry the message in a smoke signal or semaphore. For a written message the transmission medium might be a mail carrier, truck or an aeroplane. In data communication the transmission medium is usually Free space, metallic cable or fibre cable.

Guided Media: They conduct from one device to another it includes, twisted pair cable coaxial cable and fibber optic cable.

Twisted Pair Cable:

- It consists of two conductor normally copper each with its own plastic insulation twisted together.

- One of the wire is used to carry signals only as a ground reference.

- The receiver receives the difference between the two.

- Interference (noise) and cross talk may affect both wires and create unwanted signals.

- If the two wires are parallel the effect of these unwanted signals is not the same in both wires. (e.g. one is closer other is farther)

- The number of twist per unit of length (e.g. inch) has some effect on the quality of the cable.

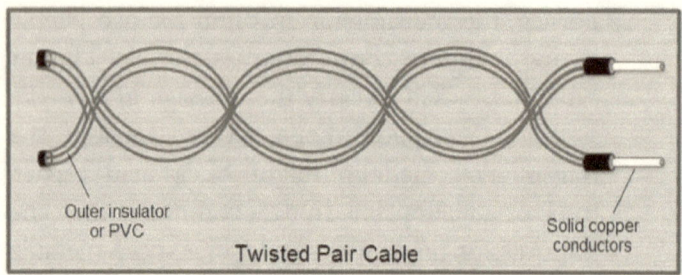

Figure 2: Twisted Pair Cable

Application:

Twisted pair cables are used in telephone lines to provide voice and data channels. DSL lines that are used by the telephone companies provide high data rate connection local area network such as IOBase-T.

COAXIAL CABLE:

- Coaxial cable or (Coax) carries signals with higher frequency range than those in twisted pair cable.

- Instead of two wires coaxial cable has a central core conductor of solid or standard wire (usually copper) enclosed in an insulating sheath which turn encased in an outer conductor of metal foil, braid or combination of the two.

- The outer metallic wrapping server both as a shield against noise and a second conductor which completes the circuit.

- The outer conductor is also enclosed in an insulating sheath and the whole cable is protected by a plastic cover.

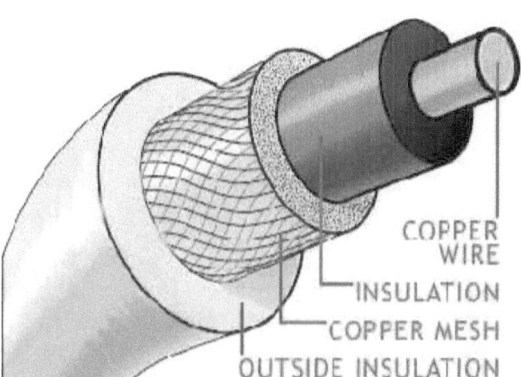

Figure 3: Coaxial Cable

Applications:

- Coaxial cable was widely used in Analog telephone networks where signal coaxial could carry 10,000 voice signals.

- It was used in digital telephone network where a single coaxial cable could carry digital data up to 60 Mbps.

- Used in cable TV network.

3.3 Fiber Optic Cable:

- Fiber-optic cable is made of glass or plastic and transmits signal in the form of light.

- To understand optical cable we must first need to explore several aspects of the nature of lights.

- Light travels in a straight line as longs as it is moving through a single uniform.

- If the ray of light traveling through one substance suddenly enters another substance the ray changes direction.

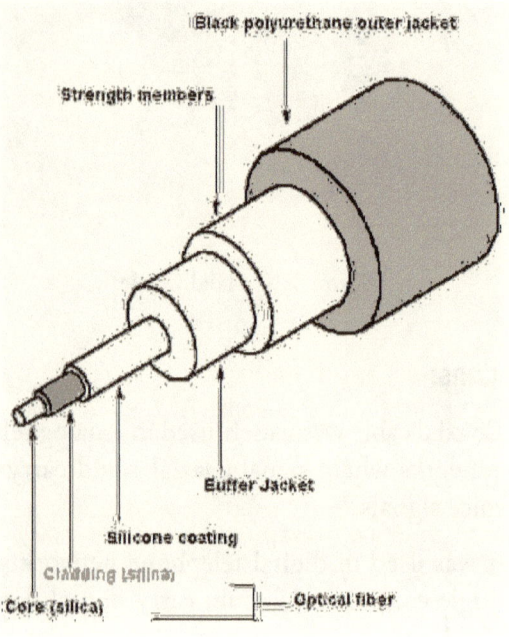

Figure 4: Fibber Optic Cable

3.4 Spread Spectrum:

- Multiplexing combines signals from several sources to achieve bandwidth efficiency.

- Spread spectrum is designed to be used in wireless application. (LAN and WAN)

- In wireless applications all stations use air (or a vacuum) as the medium of communication.

- Jamming and Interception becomes harder.
- There are two techniques to spread the bandwidth. Frequency hopping spreads spectrum and direct sequence spread spectrum.
- **Frequency hopping:** signals broad caste over seemingly random series of frequencies.
- **Direct sequence (DSS):** each bit is represented by multiple bits in transmitted signal.

3.5 Spread Spectrum Concept:

- Input fed into channel encoder produces narrow bandwidth Analog signal around central frequency.
- Signal modulated using sequence of digits.
    - spreading code/sequence
    - typically generated by pseudo noise/pseudo random number generator.
- increases bandwidth significantly.
- receiver uses same sequence to demodulate signal
- demodulated signal fed into channel decoder.

Spread Spectrum Advantage:

i. Immunity from various noise and multipath distortion.

ii. Can hide/encrypt signals.
   - Only receiver who knows spreading code can retrieve signal.

iii. Several users can share same higher bandwidth with little interference.

- Cellular telephones.
- Code division multiplexing (CDM).
- Code division multiple Access. (CDMA).

UNIT - III

CHAPTER 1

Switching

- Network is a set of connected devices whenever we have multiple devices, we have the problem of how to connect them to make one-one communication possible.
- One solution is to make a point-to-point connection between each pair of devices. (a mesh topology)
- These methods, however are impractical and wasteful when applied t a large networks.
- A switched network consists of a series of interlinked nodes called switches.
- Some of these nodes are connected to the end systems.
- Others are used only for routing.

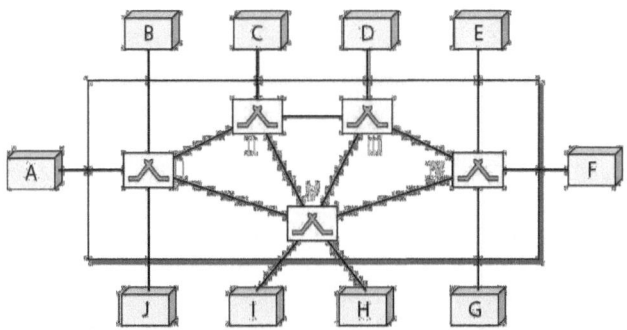

Figure 1a: Switched network

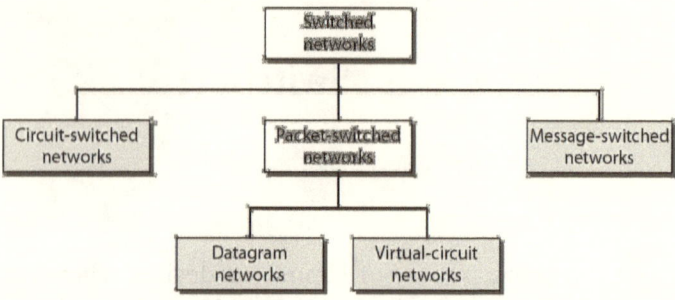

Figure 1b: Switched networks

1.1 Circuit Switched Network:

- A circuit switched network consists of a set of switches connected by physical link.
- A connection between two stations is a dedicated path made of one or more links.
- Each connection uses only one dedicated channel.
- Each link is divided into n channel.
- The end systems such as computers or telephones, are directly connected to a switch.

Three Phases:

- The actual communication in a circuit switched network requires connection setup, data transfer, and connection tear down.

Setup Phase:

- Before the two parties (or multiple parties in a conference call) can communicate, a dedicated circuit (combination of channels in links) need to be established.

- The end systems are normally connected through dedicated lines to the switches.

For e.g. in fig 8.3 when system A needs to connect to system M, it sends a setup request that includes the address of the system M to switch I. Switch I finds a channel between itself and switch IV, which finds a dedicated channel between itself and switch III.

1.2 Data Transfer Phase:

- After establishment of the dedicated circuit the two parties can transfer data.

Teardown Phase:

- When one of the party needs to disconnect a signal is sent to each switch to release the resource.

1.3 Packet Switched Network:

- The communication between two ends is done in blocks of data called packet.
- Instead of continuous communication the exchange takes place in the form of individual packets between the two computers.
- this allows us to make switches function for both storing and forwarding.
- packet is an independent entity that can be stored and sent later.

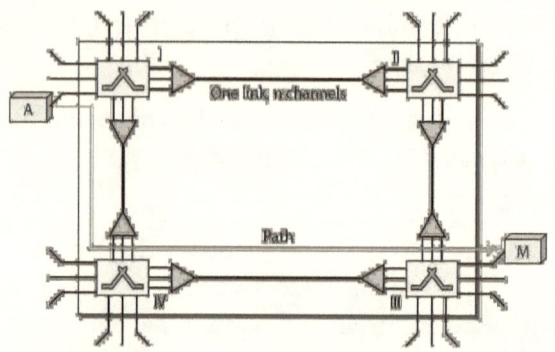

Figure 2: Packet switched network

In circuit switching, the resources need to be reserved during the setup phase the resources remain dedicated for the entire duration of data transfer until the tear down phase.

As a trivial example, let us use a circuit-switched network to connect eight telephones in a small area. Communication is through 4-kHz voice channels. We assume that each link uses FDM to connect a maximum of two voice channels. The bandwidth of each link is then 8 kHz. Figure 8.4 shows the situation. Telephone 1 is connected to telephone 7; 2 to 5; 3 to 8 and 4 to 6 Ofcourse the situation may chang when new connections are ade. The switch controls the connections.

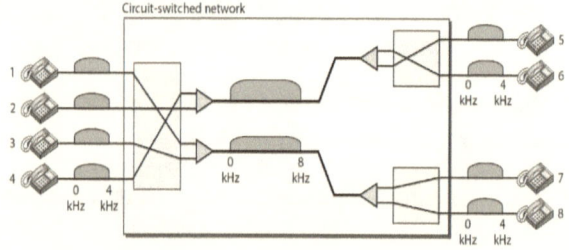

Figure 3: Circuit switched network

Example 8.2

An another example, consider circuit-switched network that connects computers in two remote offices of a private company. The offices are connected using a T-1 line leased from a communication service provider. There are two 4 × 8 (4 inputs and 8 outputs) switches in network. For each switch, four output ports are folded into the input ports to allow communication between the two offices. Figure 8.5 shows the situation.

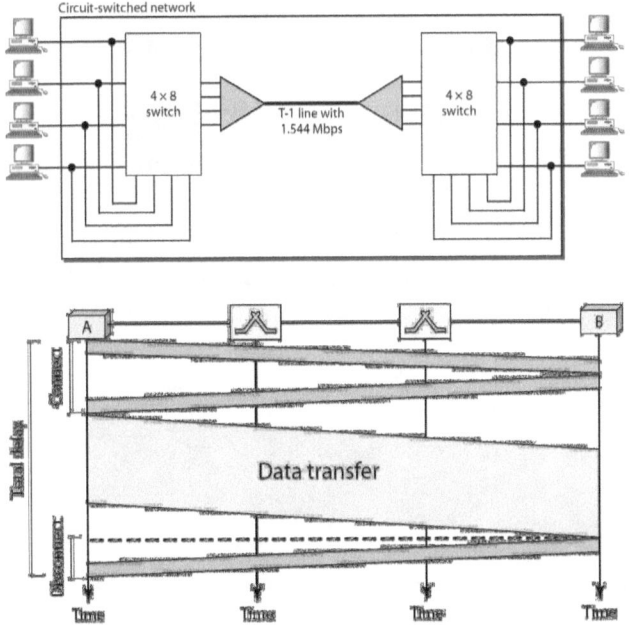

Figure 4: Delay in circuit-switched network

Switching at the physical layer in the traditional telephone network uses the circuit-switching approach.

CHAPTER 2
Datagram Network

- In data communication we need to send messages from one end system to another.

- If the message is going to pass through a packet-switched network, it needs to be divided into packets of fixed or variable size.

- In datagram each packet is treated independently.

- Packet is a part of multipack transmission.

- Packet is referred as datagram.

- Datagram switching is normally done at network layer.

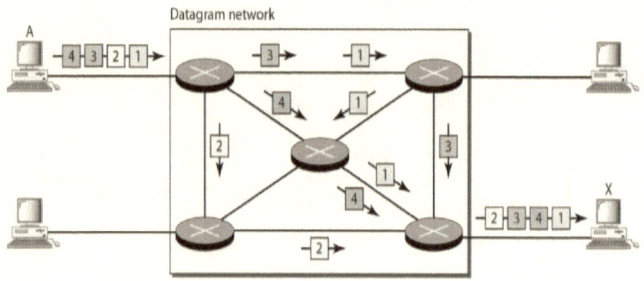

Figure 1: Used to deliver 4 packets from station x to station y

- All 4 packets (or datagrams) belong to the same message but may travel different paths to reach their destination. This is so because the link may be involved in carrying packets from other sources and do not have the necessary bandwidth to carry all packets from A to X.

- The datagram network are considered as connection less network.

2.1 Routing Table:

- If there is no setup or tear down phase, how are the packets routed to their destination in a datagram network.
- Each switch has a routing table which is based on the destination address.
- The routing table is dynamic and uploaded periodically.
- The destination addresses and the corresponding forwarding output ports are recorded in the table.

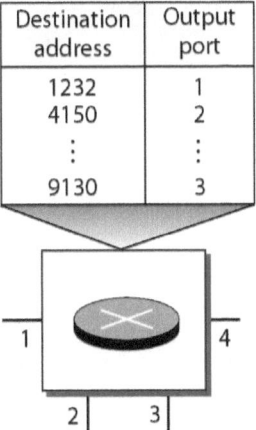

Figure 2: Routing Table

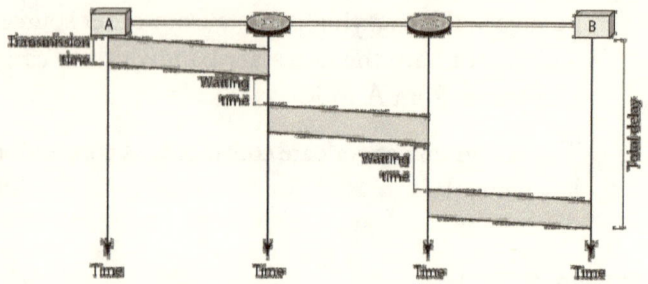

Figure 3: Delay in a datagram network

Switching in the internet is done by using the datagram approach to packet switching at the network layer.

CHAPTER 3 Virtual Circuits Networks

A virtual switched network is a cross between a circuit network and a datagram network, It has some characteristics of both.

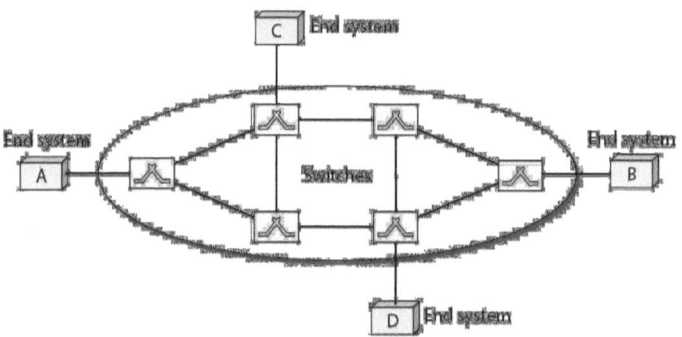

Figure 1: Virtual circuit network

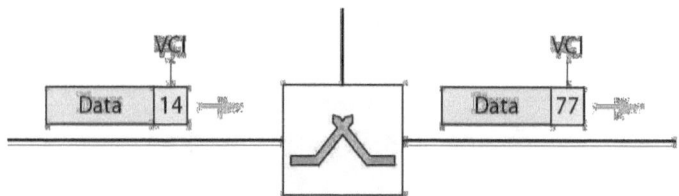

Figure 2a: Virtual-circuit Identifier

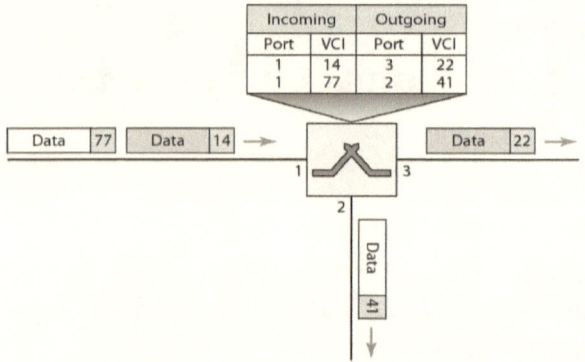

Figure 2b: Virtual circuit network

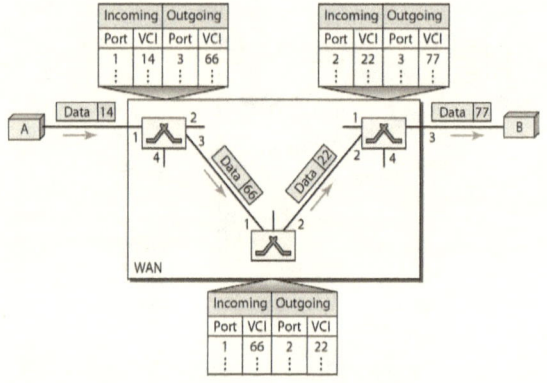

Figure 2c: Source-to-destination data transfer in a virtual-circuit

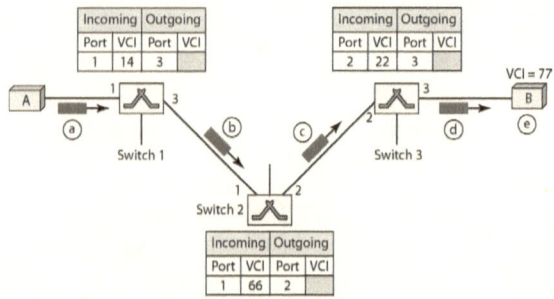

Figure 2d: Setup request in a virtual-circuit network

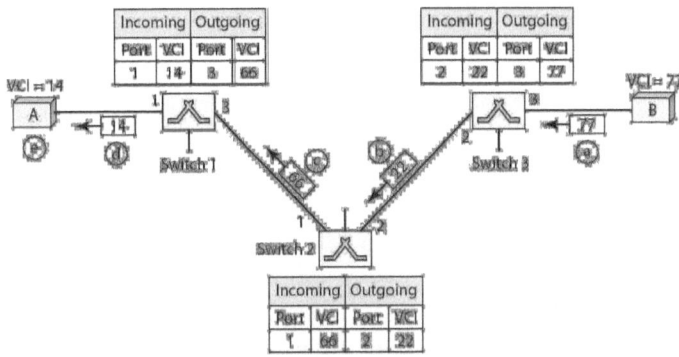

Figure 2e: Setup acknowledgment in a virtual-circuit network

In virtual-circuit switching, all packets belonging to the same source and destination travel the same path; but the packets may arrive at the destination with different delays if resource allocation is on demand.

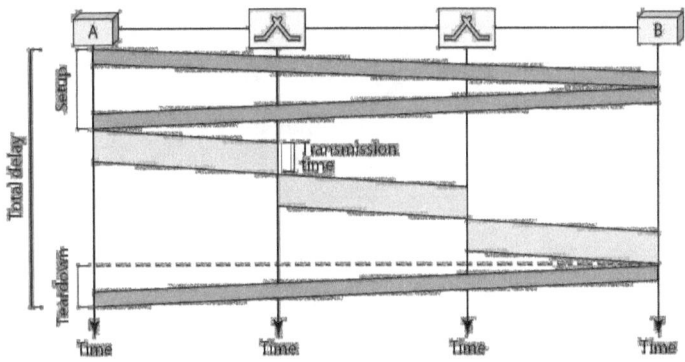

Figure 2f: Delay in a virtual–circuit network

Switching at the data link layer in switched WAN is normally implemented by using virtual-circuit techniques.

CHAPTER 4
Structure of Switch

We use switches in circuit-switched and packet-switched networks. In this section, we discuss the structures of the switches used in each type of network.

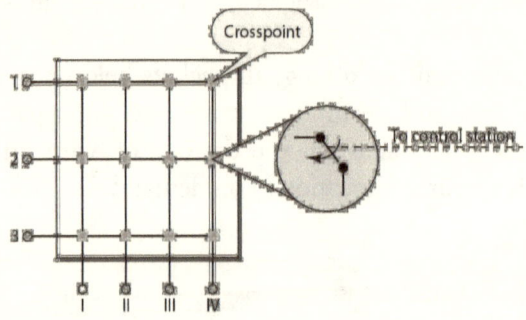

Figure 1: Crossbar switch with three inputs and four outputs

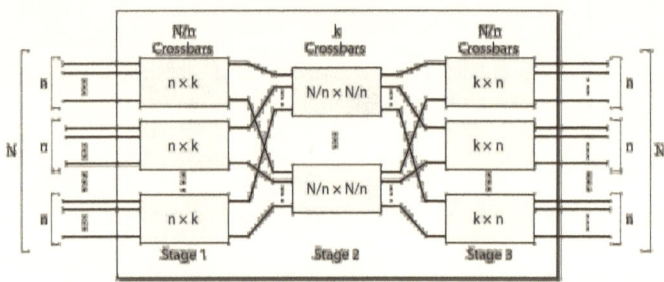

Figure 2: Multistage switch

In three stage switch, the total number of cross points is $2kN + k(N/n)2$.

Which is much smaller than the number of crosspoints in a single-stage switch (N2).

Example 8.3

Design a three-stage, 200 × 200 switch (N = 200) with k = 4 and n = 20.

Solution:

In the first stage we have N/n or 10 crossbars, each of size 20 × 4. In the second stage, we have 4 crossbars, each of size 10 × 10. In the third stage, we have 10 crossbars, each of size 4 × 20. The total number of crossbars, each of size 4 × 20. The total number of cross points is 2kN + k(N/n)2, or 2000 cross points. This is 5 percent of the number of cross points in a single-stage switch (200 × 200 = 40,000).

According to the Clos criterion

N = (N/2)1/2

k>2n−1

Cross points >= 4N[(2N)1/2−1]

Example 8.4

Redesign the previous three-stage, 200 × 200 switch using the Clos criteria with a minimum number of cross points.

Solution:

We let n = (200/2)1/2, or n = 10. We calculate k = 2n−1 = 19. In the first stage, we have 200/10, or 20, crossbars, each with 10 × 19 cross points. In the second stage, we have 19 crossbars, each with 10 × 10 cross points. In the third stage, we have 20 crossbars each with 19 × 10 cross points. The total number of cross points is 20(10 × 19) + 19(10 × 10) + 20(19 × 10) = 9500.

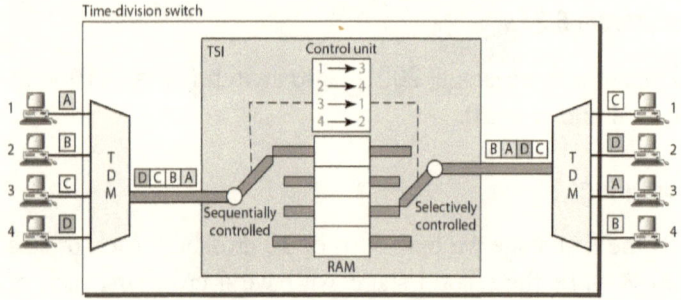

Figure 3: Time-slot interchange

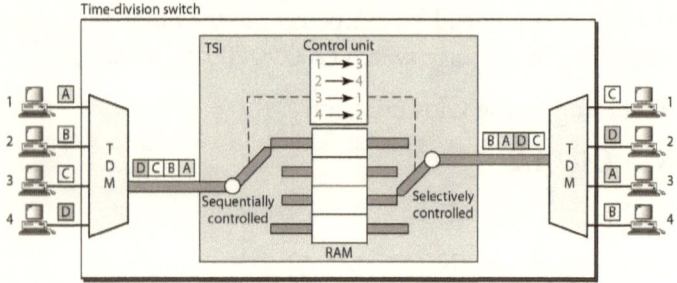

Figure 4: Time-space-time-switch

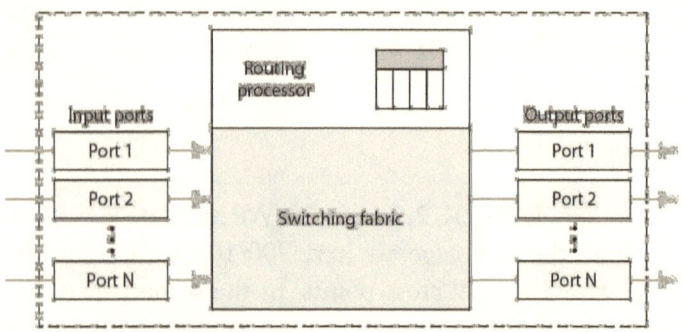

Figure 5: Packet switch components

Figure 6: Input port

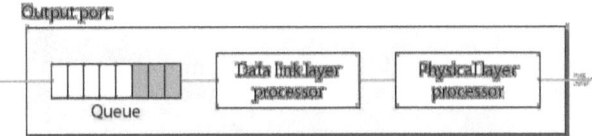

Figure 7: Output port

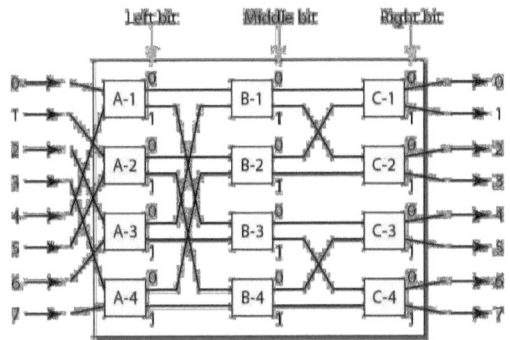

Figure 8: A banyan Switch

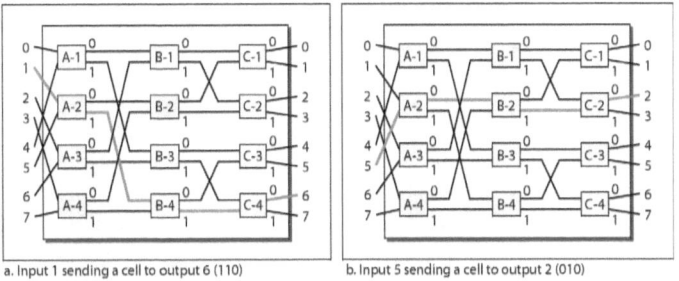

a. Input 1 sending a cell to output 6 (110)

b. Input 5 sending a cell to output 2 (010)

Figure 9: Examples of routing in a banyan switch

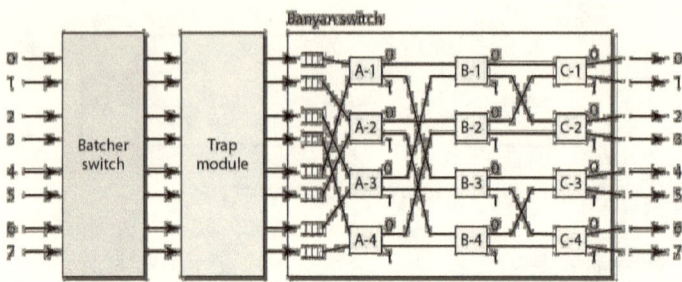

Figure 10: Batcher-banyan switch

UNIT - IV

CHAPTER 1

Data Link Layer

1.1 Data Link Layer Error Detection and Corrections:

Types of errors

1. **Single bit error:** single bit gets corrupted data becomes little error tolerable.

   | 0 | 0 | 0 | 1 |

   | 1 | 0 | 1 | 1 |

   Least likely to occur because data will be lost

   1 mbps = 1/1000000 or 1 microsec.

   Noise stays for a longer time at most impossible.

2. **Burst error:** noise stays for longer time two or more bits affected.

   Two or more bits are affected changed and corrupted.

   | 1 | 0 | 0 | 0 | 1 |

   | 1 | 1 | 0 | 0 | 0 |

Redundancy: redundancy concept is used i.e. we use extra bits to data to correct it.

1. **Error detection:** yes or no error occurred or not
2. Error correction (much more difficult) to implement why? Because exact number of bits are corrupted as well as their location.

Two things we can do when we detect error they are as follows

1. **Forward error correction:**

   We analyse the data and with the help of redundant bit we guess what is corrupted and try to fix it.

2. **Retransmission:** corruption confirmed and ask sender to resend the message.

Various Coding Scheme

1. **Block Coding**
2. **Convolution Coding**

Block Coding:

| 1 | 2 | 3 | 4 | k |

Message is divided into k blocks and add some bits

k – is the block size

r – r bit redundancy

| K | R |

N = k + r

Data	Code
00	000
01	010
10	100
11	110

Error detection table with valid code words

011 corrupted sender to receiver.

Receiver receives code word as 011 this is not existing in the table so you can say it is corrupted.

Error correction: 011 is not present so tries to correct by comparing with other entries the closest estimation.

When signal is sent ATTORTION, DISTORTION noise exist so want reliable communication device mechanism for correcting errors.

Corruption transmitted bits: longer the frame size higher the probability of single bit error, lower is the probability receiving a frame without error.

Types of Error:

Single bit error: only one bit gets changed

For eg., 1011001 → transmitted

As 1010001 → receiver

Such errors are common in parallel transmission, one line is faulty signal coming will be an error.

Burst error: more than one bit gets corrupted duration of noise is longer than the duration of one bit.

For e.g.,

Sender

1	0	1	1	0	0	1	0	1

Receiver

1	0	1	0	1	0	0	0	1

In serial transmission exposed to noise switching of some electrical signal or lightening.

Use of redundancy: additional bits are used, added to facilitate detection and correction of error.

Popular Technique:

i. Simple parity check

ii. Two dimensional parity check

iii. Check sum

iv. Cyclic redundancy check

Parity:

- it is the simplest and the most popular error detection scheme.
- appends a parity bit to the end of the data as even or odd.

e.g 1011001 → here number of ones is 4 so it is even hence add parity as 0.

1011000 0 → here number of ones is 3 so it is odd hence add parity as 1.

Asynchronous odd parity is used.

Asynchronous even parity is used.

Sender data receiver data

1011011 accept data

Compute parity check even or odd

1011011 1 if even data accept data

Transmission media — 1011011 1

compute parity bit if odd data

reject data

1.2 Performance of Simple Parity Check:

- Simple parity check can detect all single bit errors.
- It can also detect burst errors, if the number of bits in error is odd.
- The technique is not fool proof of against burst errors that inverts more than one bits. If an even number of bits are inverted due to error, the error is not detected.

Two Dimensional Parity Check:

- Performance can be improved by using two dimensional parity check, which organizes block of bits in the form of a table.
- Parity check bits are calculated for each row which is equivalent to simple parity check bit.
- Parity check bits are also calculated for all columns.
- Both are sent along with the date.
- At the receiving end these are compared with the parity bits calculated on the received data.

Example:

Original data: 10110011:10101011:01011010:11010101

Row Parity

Column Parity

Performance:

- Extra overhead is traded for better error detection capacity.
- Two dimensional parity check significantly improves error detection capability compared to simple parity check.
- It can detect many burst errors but not all.

1.3 Check Sum:

The Senders End:

- The data is divided into k segments each of m bits.
- The segments are added using 1's compliment arithmetic to get the sum.
- The sum is complemented to get the check sum.
- The check sum segment is sent along with the data segment.

The Receiver End:

- All the received segments are added using 1's complement arithmetic to get the sum.
- The sum is complemented.

- If the result zero, the received data is accepted otherwise discarded.

10110011	1
10101011	1
01011010	0
11010101	1
10010111	1

Sender example: 10110011:10101011:01011010:11010101

K = 4, m = 8

10110011

10101011

0101 1110

→ 1

010 11111

010 1 1010

---

1 0 111001

---

11 0 10101

---

1 0 001110

→ 1

1000 1 1 1 1

0111 0 0 0 0 check sum

Receiver Data

10110011

10101011

0101 1110

→ 1

---

010 11111

010 1 1010

---

1 0 111001

---

11 0 10101

---

1 0 001110

→ 1

1000 1 1 1 1

0111 0 0 0 0: sum

---

1 111 1 1 1 1

0 000 0 0 0 0: complement

Conclusion: Accept data.

Performance of check sum

- check sum detects all errors involving an odd number of bits.
- it also detects most errors involving even number of bits.

1.4 Cyclic Redundancy:

- One of the most powerful and commonly used error detecting codes.

Basic Approaches:

- Given m-bit block of bit sequence the sender generates an n-bit sequence known as a frame check sequence (FCS) so that the resulting frame, consisting of m + n bits is exactly divisible by same predetermined number.

- The receiver divides the incoming frame by that number and if there is no remainder assumes there was no error.

Message: 11100101

Polynomial: 11011(5–1 = 4) 5 is the length or size of polynomial.

XOR rule:

0 + 0 = 0

0 + 1 = 1

1 + 0 = 1

1 + 1 = 1

Example: Find CRC for the message 11100101 with the polynomial 11011.

Steps:

1. Find the length of the polynomial i.e in the e.g above it is 5, so 5–1 = 4, then you will have to add 4 zeros to the message at the sender front:

11011 √111001010000 √1010110

11011

11110

11011

10110

11011

---

1 1 010

1 1 011

0100 = CRC

DATA + CRC = 111001010100 sends to the receiver

Polynomial: 11011

11011 √111001010100 | 1010110

11011

11110

11011

10110

11011

11011

11011

00

If the answer at the receiver side is zero then there is no error in data.

1.5 Random Access Method:

- ALOHA
- Carrier Sense Multiple Access: CSMA
- Carrier Sense Multiple Access with collision Detection: CSMA/CD

ALOHA:

- The earliest random access method developed at the university of Hawaii in the early 1970's.
- Designed for a radio (wireless) Lan.
- **Simple methods.** Each station sends a frame whenever it has a frame to send.
- Since there is only one channel to show there is the possibility of collision between frame from different stations.

Pure Aloha:

- Each station sends a frame whenever it has a frame to send.
- It relies on acknowledgements from the receiver.
- If the acknowledgement does not arrive after a time out period the station resend the frame.
- Time out is equal to the max possible round trip time = $2 \times TP$.

- TP (max propagation time) time required to send a frame between the most widely separated station.

- To minimise collisions, each station waits a random amount of time (back off time to) before resending frame.

1.6 Multiple Access:

- When more than two nodes sends at the same time, the transmitted frames collide.

- All collide frames are lost and the bandwidth of the broadcast channel will be wasted.

- We need multiple access protocol to co-ordinate access to multipoint or broadcast link.

- Multi-access are needed in wire LAN's and satellite network protocols.

Multiple Access Protocol:

- Problem of controlling the access to the medium is similar to the rules of speaking in an assembly.

- Given everyone a chance to speak.

- Don't speak until you are spoken to.

- Don't monopolize the conversation.

- Revise your hand if you have a question.

- Don't interrupt when someone is speaking.

Random Access:

- In random access or contention method, no stations is superior to another station and none is assigned control over another.

- No station permits another station to send.

- At each instance a station that has data to send uses a procedure defined by the protocol to make decision on whether or not to send.

Carrier Sense Multiple Access (CSMA)

- Sense the carrier before transmit: "listen before you talk."

- CSMA can reduce the possibility of collision, but it cannot eliminate it because of the propagation delay. (a station may sense the medium and find it idle only because the first bit of a frame sent by another station has not been received)

Vulnerable Time in CSMA:

Vulnerable time is the time in which there is possibility of collision.

Vulnerable time for CSMA is the max propagation time TP needed for a signal to propagate from one end of the medium to the other.

Persistence Methods:

- When the sender (station) is ready to transmit data, it checks if the medium is busy. If so it senses the medium continually until it becomes idle.

- If the line is idle, sends the frame immediately. (with probability on 1)

Non Persistence Method:

- if a station has a frame to send, it senses the line.
- if the line is idle, the station sends the frame immediately.

1.7 Channelization:

Channelization is a multiple-access method in which the available bandwidth of a link is shared in time, frequency, or through code, between different stations. In this section, we discuss three channelization protocols.

Topics Discussed in This Section:

Frequency-Division Multiple Access (FDMA)

Time-Division Multiple Access (TDMA)

Code-Division Multiple Access (CDMA)

FDMA: Frequency Division Multiple Access:

- In frequency-division multiple access (FDMA), the available bandwidth is divided into frequency bands.
- Transmission medium is divided into M separate frequency bands.
- Each station is allocated a band to send its data.
- Each station transmits continuously on the assigned band at an average rate of R/M.

- In other words, each band is reserved for a specific station, and it belongs to the station all the time.

- A node is limited to an average rate equal R/M (where M is number of nodes) even when it is the only node with frame to be sent.

- Each station also uses a band pass filter to confine the transmitter frequencies.

- To prevent station interferences, the allocated bands are separated from one another by small guard bands.

- In FDMA, the available bandwidth of the common channel is divided into bands that are separated by guard bands.

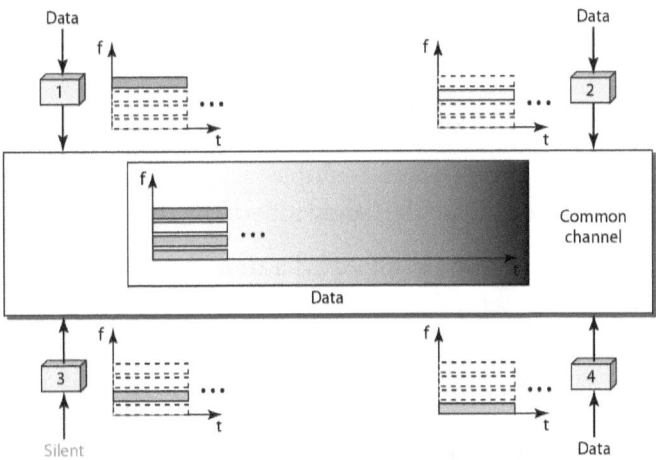

Figure 1.7: FDMA available bandwidth

- FDM is a physical layer technique that combines the loads from low-bandwidth channels and transmits them by using a high-bandwidth channel.

- The channels that are combined are low-pass.

- The multiplexer modulates the signals, combines them, and creates a band pass signal. The bandwidth of each channel is shifted by the multiplexer.

- FDMA, on the other hand, is an access method in the data link layer.

- The data link layer in each station tells its physical layer to make a band pass signal from the data passed to it. The signal must be created in the allocated band.

- There is no physical multiplexer at the physical layer. The signals created at each station are automatically band pass-filtered. They are mixed when they are sent to the common channel

1.8 TDMA: Time Division Multiple Access:

- In time-division multiple access (TDMA), the stations share the bandwidth of the channel in time.

- Each station is allocated a time slot during which it can send data.

- The entire bandwidth capacity is a single channel with its capacity shared in time between M stations

- A node must always wait for its turn until its slot time arrives even when it is the only node with frames to send.

- A node is limited to an average rate equal R/M (where M is number of nodes) even when it is the only node with frame to be sent.

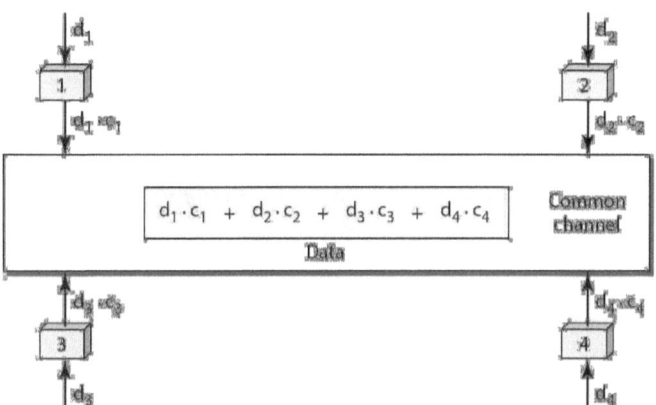

Channel

The data that go on the channel are the sum of all these terms.

Reception

- Any station that wants to receive data from one of the other three, it multiplies the data on the channel by the code of the sender.

- For example, suppose stations 1 and 2 are talking to each other. Station 2 wants to hear what station 1 is saying. It multiplies the data on the channel by c_1, the code of station 1.

Because $(c_1 \cdot c_1)$ is 4, but $(c_2 \cdot c_1)$, $(c_3 \cdot c_1)$, and $(c_4 \cdot c_1)$ are all 0s, station 2 divides the result by 4 to get the data from the station 1.

Chips

CDMA is based on coding theory. Each station is assigned a code, which is a sequence of numbers called chips.

C_1	C_2	C_3	C_4
[+1 +1 +1 +1]	[+1 −1 +1 −1]	[+1 +1 −1 −1]	[+1 −1 −1 +1]

Properties of the Chip Sequences

Each sequence is made of N elements, where N is the number of stations.

- Multiplication of a chip sequence by a scalar
    - If we multiply a sequence by a number, every element in the sequence is multiplied by that element. This is called multiplication of a sequence by a scalar.

        2 • [+1 +1 −1 −1] = [+2 +2 −2 −2]

- Multiplication of two chip sequences
    - If we multiply two equal sequences, element by element, and add the results, we get N, where N is the number of elements in each sequence. This is called the inner product of two equal sequences.

        [+1 +1 −1 −1] • [+1 +1 −1 −1] = 1 + 1 + 1 + 1 = 4

    - If we multiply two different sequences, element by element, and add the results, we get 0. This is called the inner product of two different sequences.

        [+1 +1 −1 −1] • [+1 +1 +1 +1] = 1 + 1 − 1 − 1 = 0

- Adding two sequences means adding the corresponding elements. The result is another sequence.

    [+1 +1 −1 −1] + [+1 +1 +1 +1] = [+2 +2 0 0]

- Data Representation/Encoding in CDMA.

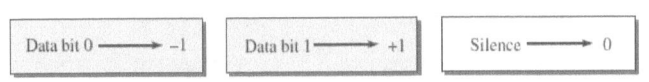

- If a station needs to send a 0 bit, it encodes it as –1;
- If it needs to send a 1 bit, it encodes it as + 1.
- When a station is idle, it sends no signal, which is interpreted as a 0.

- We assume that stations 1 and 2 are sending a 0 bit and channel 4 is sending a 1 bit. Station 3 is silent.

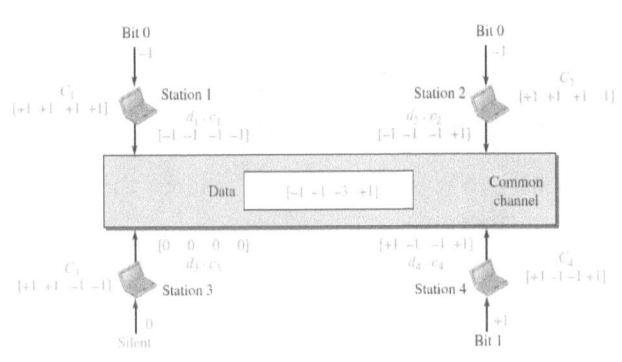

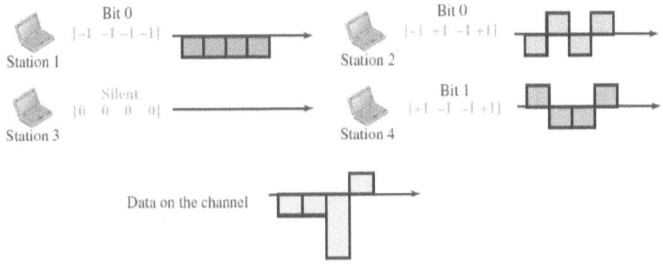

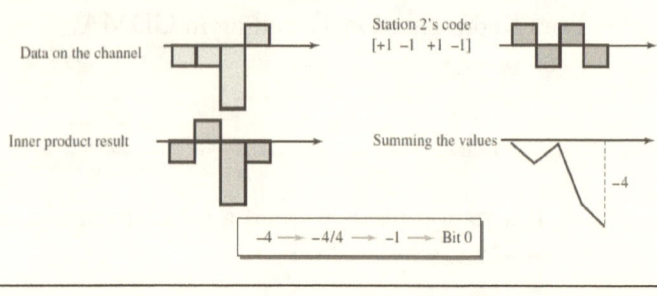

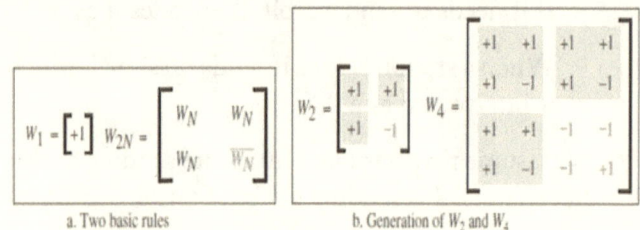

a. Two basic rules b. Generation of W_2 and W_4

Figure 1.8: General rule for creating walsh table

- The Walsh table is a two dimensional table with equal number of rows and columns.
- Each row in the Walsh table is the one chip sequence.
- The number of sequences in a Walsh table must be:

$n = 2^m$

UNIT - V

CHAPTER 1
Network Layer

1.1 IPV4 Addresses:

- it is a 32 bit address that uniquely defines the connection of a device to the Internet (for e.g. computer or a router)

- unique in the sense one and only one connection to the internet.

Address Space: It is the total number of addresses used by the protocol.

IPV4 uses 32 bit address which means address space is 232 4294, 967296, (more than 4 billion).

Notation: there are two notations to show an IPV4 address: binary notation and dotted decimal notation

Binary notation: In binary notation each octet is often referred to as byte, so it can be referred to as 32 bit address or a 4 byte address.

e.g. 01110101, 10010101, 00011101, 00000010

Dotted decimal notation: IPV4 address is made easier to read, and more compact is written in decimal form with decimal point (dot).

117.149.29.2

*Note that because each byte (octet) is 8 bits, each number in dotted decimal notation is a value ranging from 0 to 255.

128.11.3.31

↓ ↓ ↓ ↓

↓ ↓ ↓ 00011111

↓ ↓ 00000011

↓ 00001011

10000000

Change the following IPV4 address from binary notation to dotted decimal notation.

a. 10000001 00001011 00001011 11101111

   129.11.11.239

b. 11000001 10000011 00011011 11111111

   193.131.27.255

Classful Address:

IPV4 addressing the address space is divided into 5 classes A,B,C,D and E. Each class occupies some part of the address space.

- We can find the class of an address when given the address in binary notation or dotted decimal notation.

- if the address is given in decimal dotted notation the first byte defines the class.

- If the address is given in binary notation the first few bits can immediately tell us the class of the address

Classes and Blocks:

*The classful addressing wastes a large part of the address space

- Class A
- Class B
- Class C
- Class D

1.2 Structure of IPV4 Address:

Consists of Net ID and Host ID

Class	Binary	Dotted CIDR Decimal
A	111111111 0000000 0000000 0000000	255.0.0.0 /8
B	11111111 11111111 0000000 0000000	255.255.0.0/16
C	11111111 11111111 1111110000000	255.255.255.0/24

Mask:

32 bit number of contiguous 1's followed by contiguous 0's.

Helps to find net ID and the host ID

Use of IPV4 Address:

- Sub netting
  - divide large address block into smaller sub groups.
  - use of flexible net mask.
- Super netting
  - Exhausted class A and class B address space.
  - huge demand for class B address space.

Classless Addressing:

- To overcome the depletion of address space
- Restrictions:
  - The address in a block must be contiguous.
  - The number of address in a block must be power of 2.
  - The first address must be evenly divisible by the number of address.
  - consists of n consecutive 1's followed by zeros.
  - n can be any number between 0 and 32.

Tips:

- In IPV4 addressing a block of addresses can be defined as x.y.z.t/n in which x.y.z.t defines one of the addresses and /n defines the mask
- The first address in the block can be founded by setting the rightmost 32-n bits to 1's.
- The last address in the block can be found by setting the rightmost 32-n bits to 1's.
- The number of addresses in the block can be found by using the formula 232-4.

  - To combine several contiguous address spaces into a larger single address space

CHAPTER 2

IPV6

- despite all short term solutions, address depletion is still a long term problem for the internet.
- This and other problems in the IP protocol itself have been the motivation for IPV6

2.1 IPV6 Address:

- An IPV6 address is 128 bits long (16-byte).
- Hexa – decimal colon notation.
- Address

| 1111 1101 1110 1100 …… 1111111111111111 |

original FDEC:0074:0000:0000:B0FF:0000:FFF0

FDEC:74:0:0:B0FF:0:FFF0

↓

↓

FDEC:74:: B0FF:0:FFF0

↖ gap

- using this form of abbreviation 0074 can be written as 74, 000F as F, and 0000 as 0, note 3210 cannot be abbreviated.

- We can remove zero if consecutive section consists of zero replace them with double semicolon.

- this type of replacing 0 with colon is allowed only once per address.

Expand the Address:

0:15::1:12:1213

xxxx:xxxx:xxxx:xxxx:xxxx:xxxx:xxxx:xxxx

0:15:: 1:12:1213

this means the original address is

0000:0015:0000:0000:0000:0001:0012:1213

Unicast Address

- A unicast address defines a single computer

- The packet sent to a unicast address must be delivered to that specific computer.

- IPV6 defines two types of unicast address: geographically based and provider based.

- the first type is left for future definition.

- the provider based address is generally used by a normal 1 host as a unicast address.

Fields: Type ID(3-bit) Registry ID(5-bit), Provider ID(16-bit), subscriber ID(24-bit), subnet ID(32-bit), Node ID(48-bit).

3	5	provider identifier	subscriber identifier	sub net identifier	Node identifier

- **Type identifier:** this 3 bit field defines the address as a provider based address.

- **Registry identifier:** this 5 bit field indicates the agency that has registered the address. Currently three registry centres have been defined. Internic (code 11000) is the centre for North America: RIPNIC (code 01000) is centre for European Registration and APNIC (code 10100) is for Asian and pacific countries.

- **Provider identifier:** This variable length field identifies the provider for Internet access (such as ISP). A 16 bit length is recommended for this field.

- **Subscriber identifier:** When an organization subscribes to the Internet through a provider, it is assigned a subscriber identification. A 24 bit is recommended for this field.

- **Subnet Identifer:** Subnet identifier defines a specific subnetwork under under the territory of the subscriber a 32 bit length is recommended.

- **Node Identifier:** the last field identifies the node connected to the subnet. A length of 48 bit is recommended for this field to make it compatible.

2.2 Multicast Address:

- It is used to define group of host instead of one.
- A packet sent to a multicast address must be delivered to each member of the group.

8 bits 4 4 112 bits

| 11111111 | Flag | Space | Group ID |

The second field is a Flag that defines the group address as either permanent or Transient.

Permanent Address: Permanent group address is defined by the Internet Authorities and can be accessed all time.

Transient: group address is used only temporarily. The third field defines the scope of the group address.

Any Cast Address:

- Any cast address like multicast address defines the group of nodes.

- A pocket destined for any cast address is delivered to only one of the members of any cast group.

- One possible use is to assign an any cast address to all routers of an ISP that covers larger logical area in the Internet.

2.3 Process-to-Process Delivery:

- The data link layer is responsible of delivery of datagram between two neighbouring nodes over a link. This is called node-to-node delivery.

- The network layer is responsible for delivery of datagram between two hosts this is called host-to-host delivery.

- Real communication takes place between two processes (application programs) in a network this is called process-to-process delivery.

- The transport layer is responsible for process-to-process delivery.

- The transport layer is responsible for process-to-process delivery. The delivery of a packet part of a message, from one process to another.

- At transport layer we need a transport layer address called a port number to choose among multiple process running on the destination host.

- In the Internet model, the port number are 16 bit integers between 0 and 65,635.

- The client program defines itself with a port number chosen randomly by the transport layer software running on the client host. This is the ephemeral port number.

- The server process must also define itself with a port number however cannot be chosen randomly.

UNIT - VI

CHAPTER 1

UDP
(User Datagram Protocol)

- It is called connectionless, unreliable transport protocol.
- It does not add anything to the service of IP except to provide process-to-process communication instead of host-to-host.
- It is very simple protocol using minimum overhead.
- It can use UDP for sending small message with less interaction between the sender and the receiver.

1.1 User Datagram:

*UDP packets are called user datagram. They have fixed size header of 8 bytes.

*They have fixed size header of 8 bytes.

The fields are as follows:

Source Port Number:

- it is 16 bits long
- it ranges from 0–65,535.
- If the source host is client (a client sending a request)
- If the source host is server (a server is sending response)

Length:

*This is a 16 bit field that defines the total length of the user datagram header + data.

1.2 Check Sum:

*it is used to detect errors over the entire user datagram.

Uses of UDP:

- It is useful for process that requires simple request-response communication with little concern for flow and error control.
- It is suitable for process with internal flow and error control mechanism. For e.g. Trivial File Transfer Protocol (TFTP) process it includes flow and error control.

CHAPTER 2
TCP

- TCP is called Transmission control Protocol.
- It is a connection oriented protocol.
- It creates Virtual connection between two TCP's to send data.
- TCP uses flow and error control mechanism at Transport level.
- TCP is called as Connection oriented Reliable Transport Protocol.
- TCP unlike UDP is a stream oriented protocol.
- TCP allows the sending process to deliver data as a stream of bytes.
- TCP creates an environment in which the two processes seem to be connected by an imaginary tube that carries data across the Internet.
- The sending process producer (writes to) the stream of bytes and the receiving process consumer (reads from) them.

2.1 Goal of TCP Congestion Control:

- Goal of TCP is to determine the available network capacity and prevent network overload.

- Typically in discussion, First in First out queues are assumed. Congestion control work with other queuing Techniques.
- Congestion is bad for the overall performance in the network queuing Techniques.
  - Excessive delay can be caused.
  - Retransmission may result due to dropped packets.
- waste of capacity and Resources.
  - In some cases UDP Packet losses are not recovered.
  - Main reason for Packet loss is due to congestion errors are rare.

In general we can divide congestion control mechanism into two broad categories: Open-loop congestion (Prevention) and closed-loop congestion (removal).

Open Loop: It is allowed to prevent congestion before it happens.

*In this mechanism, congestion control is handled by either source or the destination. Some of the policy that can prevent congestion are:

1. **Retransmission Policy:** To retransmit packet.
2. **Window Policy:** Tries to send specific packet that have been lost.
3. **Acknowledgement Policy:** A receiver may decide to Acknowledge only N packets at a time.

2.2 Closed-Loop Congestion Control:

*Mechanism tries to alleviate congestion after it happens.

Back Pressure:

*The technique of back pressure refers to a congestion control mechanism in which congested node stops receiving data from the immediate upstream node or nodes.

2.3 Choke Packet:

*In choke packet method the warning is from the router which has encountered congestion to the source station directly.

Implicit Signalling:

*There is no communication between the congested node or the nodes and the source.

2.4 Explicit Signalling:

*The node that experiences congestion can explicitly send a signal to the source or destination.

Backward Signalling:

*A bit is set in a packet moving in the direction of congestion. This bit can warn the source that there is congestion.

Forward Signalling:

*A bit is set in a packet moving in the direction of the congestion. This bit can warn the destination that there is a congestion.

UNIT - VII

CHAPTER 1 Application Layer

DNS: Domain name system. It takes the names we type into a web browser and resolves them to a proper network address.

- DNS consists of name servers and resolvers.
- DNS stores authoritative data about sections of a distributed data base and respond to browser requests by supplying name address conversions.
- There are several implementations of DNS.
- one of the most popular is called BIND.
- Bind is an internet name server for UNIX OS.
- The last portion of a host name, such as.COM is the top-level domain to which the host belongs.
- Within every top level domain there is second level domain, such as novell.Com
- The fully qualified Domain name (FQDN) consists of the host name appended to the computers domain.
- At the top of the DNS database tree or root name servers contain pointer records to master name servers for each of the top-level domains.

- Each name server messages a group of records called a zone.

- Zones are set up to help resolve names more easily and for replication purposes.

- DNS Zones specify the domain name boundary in which a DNS server has authority to perform name Translations.

- The .arpa domain maintains a reverse list of IP addresses to Internet addresses.

- The IP addresses in the .arpa domain are listed in reverse order.

- You can either administer your own DNS servers or have a Internet Service Provider (ISP) do it for you.

1.1 Telnet:

- Telnet is a protocol that provides a way for clients to connect to servers on the Internet.

- The Telnet application is built over TCP/IP and provides the local machine with the means to evaluate a Terminal session compatible with the remote computer.

- It allows the user to create a connection and send commands instructions interactively to the remote machines.

- Telnet has no graphical user interface (GUI).

- The Telnet TCP connection is established between a random unprivileged port on the client and port 23 on the server.

- Because a TCP connection is full-duplex and identified by the pair of ports, the server can engage in many simultaneous connections involving its port 23 and different random unprivileged ports on the client.

1.2 FTP:

- File transfer protocol allows a person to transfer files between two computers.
- This is usually a client and a server.
- FTP makes it possible to move one or more files between computers with security and data Integrity controls appropriate for the Internet.
- FTP is a TCP-based service that utilizes a data port and a control port.
- Traditionally these are Port 21 for the command port and port 20 for the data port.
- In active mode, FTP client doesn't make the actual connection to the data port of the server, it simply states what port it is listening on and the server connects to the specified port on the client.
- In passive mode the client initiates all connections to the server.
- The client opens two random unprivileged ports locally.
- This is useful when trying to provide FTP connections through firewalls.
- Most browsers support only passive mode.

- It is used in standard routing, the route table is consulted every time a frame is received and so plays fundamental role in the proper delivery of data.

- A routing table only maintains the best possible route to a destination, not all possible routes.

- It is used with web browser or through a command prompt.

- programs such as Fetch, Cute FTP, and WS_FTP also are used for transferring and managing files.

- TRICKLE provides an alternative to FTP.

- It distributes files by request or by subscription.

1.3 SNMP:

- It is simple network management protocol.

- It is a part of TCP/IP protocol suite.

- It is an application layer protocol that is used to exchange management information between network devices.

- It enables network administrators to manage network performance, find and solve network problems, and plan for network growth.

- SNMP management infrastructure consists of three main components.
    - SNMP Managed node.
    - SNMP agent.
    - SNMP network management station.

- Three versions of SNMP exist.
- SNMPV3 addresses major security and authentication concerns of SNMPV1 and SNMPV2.
- All agents and management station must belong to an SNMP community.
- SNMP and management stations that belong to the same community can accept messages from each other.
- The Remote monitoring (RMON) specification can be considered an extension to the SNMP standard.
- CISCO system includes SNMP and RMON functionality in its software.

CHAPTER 2: Quality of Service (QoS)

- it is the description or measurement of the overall performance of a service, like telephony, or computer network, or a cloud computing services.

- network service based on the quality is often considered as packet loss, bit rate, throughput, transmission delay, availability, jitter etc.

- in the field of computer networking and other packet-switched telecommunication networks, quality of service refers to traffic prioritization and resource reservation control mechanisms rather than the achieved service quality.

- quality of service is the ability to provide different priority to different applications, users or data flows.

- quality of service is particularly important for the transport of traffic with special requirements.

- in packet switched networks, quality of service is affected by various factors, which can be divided into human and technical factors.

- human factors include: stability of service quality, availability of service, waiting times and user information.

- Technical factors include: reliability, scalability, effectiveness, maintainability and network congestion.

Many things can happen to packets as they travel from origin to destination, resulting in the following problems as seen from the point of view of the sender and receiver:

Good Put:

Due to varying load from disparate users sharing the same network resources, the maximum throughput that can be provided to a certain data stream may be too low for real-time multimedia services.

Packet Loss:

The network may fail to deliver (*drop*) some packets due to network congestion. The receiving application may ask for this information to be retransmitted, possibly resulting in congestive collapse or unacceptable delays in the overall transmission.

Errors

Sometimes packets are corrupted due to bit errors caused by noise and interference, especially in wireless communications and long copper wires. The receiver has to detect this and, just as if the packet was dropped, may ask for this information to be retransmitted.

Latency

It might take a long time for each packet to reach its destination because it gets held up in long queues, or it takes a less direct route to avoid congestion. In some cases, excessive latency can render an application such as VoIP or online gaming unusable.

Packet Delay Variation

Packets from the source will reach the destination with different delays. A packet's delay varies with its position in the queues of the routers along the path between source and destination and this position can vary unpredictably. Delay variation can be absorbed at the receiver but in so doing increases the overall latency for the stream.

Out-of-Order Delivery

When a collection of related packets is routed through a network, different packets may take different routes, each resulting in a different delay. The result is that the packets arrive in a different order than they were sent. This problem requires special additional protocols for rearranging out-of-order packets. The reordering process requires additional buffering ant the receiver and as with packet delay variation increases the overall latency for the stream.

References

[AL98] Albitz, P. and Liu, C. DNS and BIND. Sebastopol, CA: O'Reilly, 1998.

[AZ03] Agrawal D. and Zeng, Q. Introduction to Wireless and Mobile Systems. Pacific Grove, CA, NJ: Brooks/Cole Thomson Learning, 2003.

[Bar02] Barr, T, Invitation to Cryptology. Upper Saddle River, NJ: Prentice Hall, 2002.

[BELOO] Bellamy, J. Digital Telephony. New York, NY: Wiley, 2000.

[Ber96J Bergman, J. Digital Baseband Transmission and Recording. Boston, MA: Kluwer, 1996.

[Bis03] Bishop, M. Computer Security. Reading, MA: Addison-Wesley, 2003.

[BlaOO] Black, U. QoS In Wide Area Network. Upper Saddle River, NJ: Prentice Hall, 2000.

[81a03] Blahut, R. Algebraic Codesfor Data Transmission. Cambridge, UK: Cambridge University Press, 2003

[CBR03] Cheswick, W., Bellovin, S., and Rubin, A. Firewalls and Internet Security. Reading, MA: Addison-Wesley, 2003.

[ComOO] Comer, D. Internetworking with TCPlIp, Volume 1: Principles, Protocols, and

Architecture. Upper Saddle River, NJ: Prentice Hall, 2000

[Com04] Comer, D. Computer Networks. Upper Saddle River, NJ: Prentice Hall, 2004.

[CouO1] Couch, L. Digital and Analog Communication Systems. Upper Saddle River, NJ: Prentice Hall, 2000.

[DH03] Doraswamy, H. and Harkins, D. IPSec. Upper Saddle River, NJ: Prentice Hall, 2003.

[Dro02] Drozdek, A. Elements of Data Compression. Brooks/Cole Thomson Learning, 2003.

[DutO1] Dutcher, D. The NAT Handbook. New York, NW: Wiley, 2001.

[FH98] Ferguson, P. and Huston, G. Quality o/Service. NewYork, NW: Wiley, 1996.

[For03] Forouzan, B. Local Area Networks. New York, NY: McGraw-Hill, 2003.

[For06] Forouzan, B. TCPIIP Protocol Suite. New York, NY: McGraw-Hill, 2006.

[FRE96] Freeman, R. Telecommunication System Engineering. New York, NW:

[GarO1] Garret, P. Making, Breaking Codes. Upper Saddle River, NJ: Prentice Hall, 2001.

[Gas02] Gast, M. 802.11 Wireless Network. Sebastopol, CA: O'Reilly, 2000.

[GW04] Garcia, A. and Widjaja, I, Communication Networks. New York, NY: McGraw-Hill, 2003.

[HalO1] Halsall, F. Multimedia Communication. Reading, MA: Addison-Wesley, 2001. [Ham80]

[Hsu03] Hsu, H. Analog and Digital Communications. New York, NY: McGraw-Hill, 2003.

[HuiOO] Huitema, C. Routing in the Internet. Upper Saddle River, NJ: Prentice Hall, 2000.

[IzzOO] Izzo, P. Gigabit Networks. New York, NY: Wiley, 2000.

[Jam03] Jamalipour, A. Wireless Mobile Internet. New York, NY: Wiley, 2003.

[KCK98] Kadambi, j., Crayford, I., and Kalkunte, M. Gigabit Ethernet. Upper Saddle River, NJ: Prentice Hall, 1998.

[Kei02] Keiser, G. Local Area Networks. New York, NY: McGraw-Hill, 2002.

[Kes97] Keshav, S. An Engineering Approach to Computer Networking. Reading, MA: Addison Wesley, 1997.

[KMK04] Kumar A., Manjunath, D., and Kuri, 1. Communication Networking. San Francisco, CA: Motrgan, Kaufmans, 2004.

[KPS02] Kaufman, c., Pedmann, R., and Speciner, M. Network Security. Upper Saddle River, NJ: Prentice Hall, 2000.

[KROS] Kurose, 1. and Ross, K. Computer Networking. Reading, MA: Addison Wesley, 2005.

[Los04] Loshin, P. IPv6: Theory, Protocol, and Practice. San Francisco, CA: Morgan, Kaufmans, 2001.

[Mao04] Mao, W. Modem Cryptography. Upper Saddle River, NJ: Prentice Hall, 2004.

[Max99] Maxwell, K. Residential Broadband. New York, NY: Wiley, 2003.

[MOV97] Menezes, A., Oorschot, P and Vanstone, S. Handbook of Applied Cryptograpy. New York, NY: CRC Press, 1997.

[Moy 98] Moy, J. OSPF: Anatomy ofan Internet Routing Protocol. Reading, MA Addison-Wesley, 1998.

[MSOl] Mauro D. and Schmidt K. Essential SNMP Sebastopol, CA: O'Reilly, 2001.

[PD03] Peterson, L., and Davie B. Computer Networks: A Systems Approach. San Francisco, CA: Morgan, Kaufmans, 2000.

[Pea92] Pearson, J. Basic Communication Theory. Upper Saddle River, NJ: Prentice Hall,' 1992.

[PerOO] Perlman, R. Interconnection: Bridges, Routers, Switches, and Intemet working Protocols. Reading, MA: Addison-Wesley, 2000.

[PHS03] Pieprzyk, J., Hardjono, T, and Seberry, J, Fundamentals of Computer Security. Berlin, Germany: Springer, 2003.

[ResOl] Rescorla, E. SSL and TSL. Upper Saddle River, NJ: Prentice Hall, 2000.

[Rhe03] Rhee, M, Internet Security. New York, NY: Wiley, 2003.

[Ror96] Rorabaugh, C. Error Coding Cookbook. New York, NY: McGraw-Hill, 1996.

[SaI03] Solomon, D. Data Privacy and Security. Berlin, Germany: Springer, 2003.

[Sau98] Sauders, S. Gigabit Ethernet Handbook. New York, NY: McGraw-Hill, 1998.

[Sch96] Schneier, B. Applied Cryptography. Reading, MA: Addison-Wesley, 1996.i.

[Sch03] Schiller, B. Mobile Communications. Reading, MA: Addison-Wesley, 2003.

[Spi74] Spiegel, M. FourierAnalysis. New York, NY: McGraw-Hill, 1974.

[SpuOO] Spurgeon, C. Ethernet. Sebastopol, CA: O'Reilly, 2000.

[S8805] Shimonski, R., Steiner, R. Sheedy, S. Network Cabling Illuminated. Sudbury, MA: Jones and Bartlette, 2005.

[8ta02] Stallings, W. Wireless Communications and Networks. Upper Saddle River, NJ: Prentice Hall, 2002.

[Sta03] Stallings, W. Cryptography and Network Security. Upper Saddle River, NJ: Prentice Hall, 2003.

[8ta04] Stallings, W. Data And Computer Communications. Upper Saddle River, NJ: Prentice Hall, 2004.

[S1398] Stallings, W. High Speed Networks. Upper Saddle River, NJ: Prentice Hall, 1998.

[Ste94] Stevens, W. TCPIIP Illustrated, Volume 1. Upper Saddle River, NJ: Prentice Hall, 2000.

[Ste96] Stevens, W. TCPIIP Illustrated, Volume 3. Upper Saddle River, NJ: Prentice Hall, 2000.

[Ste99] Stewart III, J. BGP4: Inter-Domain Routing in the Internet. Reading, MA: Addison-Wesley, 1999.

[Sti02] Stinson, D. Cryptography. New York, NY: Chapman & Hall/CRC, 2002.

[SubOl] Subramanian, M. Network Management. Reading, MA: AddisonWesley, 2000.

[SWE99] Scott, C., Wolfe, P, and Erwin, M. Virtual Private Networks. Sebastopol, CA: O'Reilly, 1998.

[Sti02] Stinson, D. Cryptography. New York, NY: Chapman & Hall/CRC, 2002.

[SubO1] Subramanian, M. Network Management. Reading, MA: AddisonWesley, 2000.

[SWE99] Scott, C., Wolfe, P, and Erwin, M. Virtual Private Networks. Sebastopol, CA: O'Reilly, 1998.

[SX02] Stewart, R. and Xie, Q. Stream Control Transmission Protocol (SCTP) Reading, MA: Addison-Wesley, 2002.

[Tan03] Tanenbaum, A. Computer Networks. Upper Saddle River, NJ: Prentice Hall, 2003.

[Tho00] Thomas, S. SSL and TLS Essentials. New York, NY: Wiley, 2000.

[WV00] Warland, J. and Varaiya, P. High Peiformance Communication Networks. San Francisco, CA: Morgan, Kaufmans, 2000.

[WZO1] Wittmann, R. and Zitterbart, M. Multicast Communication. San Francisco, CA: Morgan, Kaufmans, 2001.

[YSO1] Yuan R. and Strayer, W. Virtual Private Network. Reading, MA: AddisonWesley, 2001.

[Zar02] Zaragoza, R. The Art ofError Correcting Coding. Reading, MA: Addison-Wesley, 2002.

[BAF07] Behrouz A Forouzan: Datat Communications and Networking 4th edition network models (McGraw-Hill Professional 2007).

www.ingramcontent.com/pod-product-compliance
Lightning Source LLC
Chambersburg PA
CBHW030809180526
45163CB00003B/1206